In the Name of Allah, the Gracious, the Merciful

Judgment on Interest Analysed in Qur'aanic Light

by
Mohammad Shafi

Introduction

On 14 Ramadan 1420 (Hijri), the Shariah Appellate Bench of the Supreme Court of Pakistan gave its decision banning interest in all its forms and by whatever name it may be called.

The Shariah Appellate Bench consisted of 1) Mr. Justice Khalil-ur-Rahman, 2) Mr. Justice Munir A Shaikh, 3) Mr. Justice Wajeehuddin Ahmad, and 4) Maulana Justice Muhammad Taqi Usmani.

The full judgment of the court consists of about 1100 pages. The main part of the judgment was written by Mr. Justice Khalil-ur Rahman (550 pages) and Maulana Justice Mufti Taqi Usmani (250 pages). A note of 98 pages was written by Mr. Justice Wajeehuddin Ahmad. The order of the court consists of 106 pages.

I reproduce here the text written by Maulana Justice Taqi Usmani. It has been copied from the site http://www.albalagh.net/Islamic_economics/riba_judgement.shtml

Although this Judgement has been pronounced by the highest Court in Pakistan, that Court is not the final Authority in Islam. Being human beings after all, the learned judges are prone to errors/mistakes.

And if we treat the judgement as sacrosanct or absolutely devoid of any error, we raise the human judges to the status of the Almighty Allah, Who alone can make no mistakes! We would thus commit *Shirk*, an unpardonable sin!

It is therefore our bounden duty to check this judgment too on the divine Touchstone - the Qur'aan. I have attempted to do just that, here. My comments, wherever called for in the light of the Holy Book, are given in blue font within the text of the judgement.

Mohammad Shafi
19th September, 2008
Mumbai, INDIA

CONTENTS OF THE JUDGMENT

An Objective Study of the Qur'anic Verses Dealing with *Riba*
MyComments 1
- Historical Analysis of the Verses of *Riba*
- Surah Ar-Rum
- Surah An-Nisaa
My Comments 2
- Surah Al-i-'Imran
My Comments 3
My Comments 4
- The Time of Prohibition of *Riba*
My Comments 5
- The Last Verse of the Qur'an
- What is Meant by *Riba*?
My Comments 6
- *Riba* in the Bible
My Comments 7
- The Definition of *Riba* as given by the Exegetes of the Holy Qur'an
- The Detailed Account of *Riba al-Jahiliyya*
My Comments 8
- The Statement of Sayyidna Umar, Radi-Allahu anhu, About the Ambiguity in the Concept of Riba
My Comments 9
- A Description of Riba al-Fadl
- The Correct Meaning of Sayyidna Umar's Statement
My Comments 10
- Productive or Consumption Loans
- Validity of a Transaction is not Based on the Financial Status of a Party
- The Nature of Qur'anic Prohibitions

- Banking and Productive Loans in the Age of Antiquity

- Commercial Interest in Arabia
My Comments 11
- Excessive Rates of Interest
My Comments 12
- Riba al-Fadl and Bank loans
My Comments 13
- The Jurisdiction of this Court in the Laws of Interest
- Basic Cause of Prohibition
- The Difference between Illat and Hikmat
My Comments 14
- Rationale of the Prohibition of Riba
- Nature of Money
My Comments 15
- The Nature of Loan
My Comments 16
- Overall Effects of Interest
- Evil Effects on Allocation of Resources
- Evil Effects on Production
- Evil Effects on Distribution
- Expansion of Artificial Money and Inflation
My Comments 17
- Interest and Indexation
My Comments 18
- Mark-up and Interest
My Comments 19
- Qarz and Qiraz
- Riba and Doctrine of Necessity
- Domestic Transactions
- Profit and Loss Sharing
- Some Objections on Musharakah Financing
- Risk of Loss
- Dishonesty

- Mudarabahah Transaction
- The Loans of the Government
- Foreign Loans
My Comments 20
- Conclusions
My Conclusions

The Text of the Judgment

1. All these appeals arise out of the same judgment of the learned Federal Shariat Court dated 14 November 1991, whereby the Court has declared a number of laws of the country repugnant to the Injunctions of Islam as they have provided for charging or paying interest, which according to the findings of the learned Federal Shariat Court, falls within the definition of *riba* clearly prohibited by the Holy Qur'an.

2. The basic issues involved in all these appeals being similar, all of them were heard together and are being disposed of by this single judgment.

3. Most of the appellants as well as some juris-consults argued before us that interest-based commercial transactions were invented by the modern business, and their history does not go back more than 400 years, therefore they are not covered by the term '*riba*' used by the Holy Qur'an, and the prohibition of *riba* does not include the prohibition of interest as in vogue in modern transactions.

4. This view is sought to be supported by five different lines of argument adopted before us against the prohibition of interest.

5. The first approach to interpret the term *riba*, as adapted by some of the appellants, was that the verses of the Holy Qur'an which prohibit *riba* were revealed in the last days of the life of the Holy Prophet, Sall-Allahu alayhi wa sallam, and he did not have an opportunity to interpret them properly and therefore no hard and fast definition of the term

riba can be found in the Holy Qur'an or in the Sunnah of the Holy Prophet, Sall-Allahu alayhi wa sallam. Since the term remained ambiguous in nature, it falls within the area of *Mutashabihat* and its correct meaning is unknown. According to this approach the prohibition of *riba* should he restricted to the limited transactions expressly mentioned in the Hadith literature and the principle cannot be extended to the modern banking system which was not even imaginable at the time of revelation of the verses.

6. The second line of argument runs on the basis that the word '*riba*' refers only to the usurious loans on which an excessive rate of interest used to be charged by the creditors which would entail exploitation. As far the modern banking interest, it cannot be termed as '*riba*' if the rate of interest is not excessive or exploitative.

7. The third argument differentiates between consumption loans and commercial loans. According to this approach the word "*Al-Riba*" used in the Holy Qur'an is restricted to the increased amount charged on the consumption loans used to be taken by the poor people for their day to day needs. These poor people deserved sympathetic attitude on humanitarian grounds, but the rich people exploited their miserable condition to charge heavy amounts from them in the form of usury. The Holy Qur'an has taken this practice as a severe offence against humanity and declared war against those involved in such abominated transactions. So far as the modern commercial loans are concerned, they were neither in vogue in the days of the Holy Prophet, Sall-Allahu alayhi wa sallam, nor has the

Holy Qur'an addressed them while prohibiting *'riba'*. Even the basic philosophy underlying the prohibition of ' *riba* ' cannot be applied to these commercial and productive loans where the debtors are not poor people. In most cases they are wealthy or at least economically well-off and the loans taken by them are generally used for generating profits. Therefore, any increase charged from them by the creditors cannot he termed as *Zulm* (injustice) which was the basic cause of the prohibition of *'riba'*.

8. The fourth theoryadvanced during the arguments was that the Holy Qur'an has prohibited *riba-al-jahiliyya* only which, according to a number of traditions, was a particular transaction of loan where no additional amount over and above the principal was stipulated in the agreement of loan. However, if the debtor could not pay off the loan at its due date, the creditor would give him more time against charging an additional amount. According to this theory, if an increased amount is stipulated in the initial agreement of loan, it does not constitute *riba al-Quran*. However, it does fall in the definition of *riba-al-fadl*, prohibited by the Sunnah. Its prohibition is of a lesser degree which can be termed as makrooh and not haram. Therefore, this prohibition may be relaxed in cases of genuine need and it does not apply to the non-Muslims. Being a special law applicable to the Muslims only, it falls within the category of 'Muslim Personal Law', which falls outside the jurisdiction of the Federal Shariat Court, as contemplated in Article 203(B) of the Constitution of Pakistan.

9. The fifth way of argument was that although the modern interest-based transactions are covered by the prohibition of ' *riba* ', yet the commercial interest being the back-bone of the modern economic activities throughout the world, no country can live without being involved in interest-based transactions and it will be a suicidal act to abolish interest from domestic and foreign transactions. Islam, being a practical religion, recognizes the principle of necessity and it has allowed even to eat pork in extreme situation where one cannot live without eating it. The same principle of necessity should be applied to the interest-based transactions also, and on the basis of this necessity the laws permitting the charge of interest should not be declared repugnant to the injunctions of Islam.

10. All these different sets of arguments led us to resolve the main issue i.e. whether or not commercial interest of modern financial system falls within the definition of *riba* prohibited by the Holy Qur'an, and if it does, whether they can he allowed on the basis of necessity. This also led us to examine whether the modern financial transactions can be designed without interest and whether or not the proposed alternatives are feasible keeping in view the modern structure of commerce and finance. In order to resolve these issues we invited a number of experts as juris-consults consisting of Shariah scholars, economists, bankers, accountants and representatives of modern business and trade who have provided assistance to the Court in their respective areas of specialization.

Back to Top

An Objective Study of the Qur'anic Verses Dealing with *Riba*

11. Before analyzing the above-mentioned arguments, let us undertake an objective study of the verses of the Holy Qur'an about *riba*. There are four different sets of verses which were revealed on different occasions.

12. First, in Surah Ar-Rum, a Makkan Surah wherein the term *riba* finds mention in the following words:

وَمَآ ءَاتَيْتُم مِّن رِّبًا لِّيَرْبُوَاْ فِىٓ أَمْوَٰلِ ٱلنَّاسِ فَلَا يَرْبُواْ عِندَ ٱللَّهِ

> "And whatever *riba* you give so that it mayincrease in the wealth of the people, it does not increase with Allah." [Ar-Rum 30:39]

My Comments 1: This is the first verse, in order of revelation, in the matter of *Ar-Riba*, which later gets prohibited. As such, if the term needed any defining or explaining, this verse would be the most apprpriate one wherein to do it. But, unfortunately, the learned Judge has not given it the due deliberation it deserves.

In the original Arabic text, the verse begins with the words *Wa maa aataytum*. The plain literal translation of this phrase would be: 'And that which you give'. The Arabic words immediately following this phrase are *min riban*. The preposition *min* could have several meanings according to the context in which it is used. Here it is used in the context of, or as a preposition to, the word *riban*. The same preposition has been used again, in the latter part of the verse, in the context of the word *zakaatin*.

There is no controversy as regards *zakaat*. The universally accepted meaning of this word is 'charity'. The words *min zakaatin* may therefore naturally be translated as 'in charity', 'by way of charity' or 'for charity'. And since the Arabic preposition has been used in the same fashion in the phrase *Wa maa aataytum min riban,* it (the phrase) may be translated as 'And that which you give, in, by way of or for *riba'*. The learned Judge, however, has not taken any cognizance of the preposition *min* in this phrase, thus rendering the meaning of the verse, as given by him, confusing and unclear!

In this Judgement, the learned Judge has concluded that *riba* mentioned in the verse here is 'interest' as we understand this English word now. So if we substitute the Arabic word with the English meaning the Judge has given it, his complete rendering in English would be: **"And whatever interest you give so that it may increase in the wealth of the people, it does not increase with Allah."** This rendering, as anyone can see, makes no proper sense.

Had the learned Judge taken the Arabic preposition into account, his English rendering could have been: **"And whatever you give on interest, so that it may increase in the wealth of**

the people, it does not increase with Allah." Such a rendering could of course make some sense, but not a logical one!

Because, there are Banks in the present day world who charge interest at rates calculated to cover just their expenses plus their reasonable profit. The Banks are entitled to such profit for the work they do in providing purchasing power (money) to people and institutions needing it - a service necessary to mankind. Interest, as such, is the Bank's own wealth - and not of the debtors! By interpreting *riba* as interest, therefore, the learned Judge has, *nauzubillah*, made the divine verse look like being self-contradictory! Every right thinking Muslim has to reject such interpretation as being *ultra vires* the Qur'aan.

It is to be noted that the word *riba* as used in this verse is without the Arabic definite article *al*. And, in verses subsequently revealed, it is used with the article prefixed to it. It is also to be noted that it is *Al-Riba* (pronounced as *Ar-Riba*) - and not *Riba* as such - that gets specifically prohibited in verse 2.275.

In these circumstances, it is but natural to take the word *riba* used in verse 30.39 in its literal meaning of increase, growth, gain or profit. Allah Ta'ala, in His infinite wisdom, has helped us in understanding the meaning of the word thus by giving us its verb form *yarbu* undoubtedly meaning 'increase', later in the very same verse.

And the context of the verse suggests that the phrase *Wa maa aataytum minriban* may most appropriately be translated as 'And that which you give for profit'.

The learned Judge has quoted and rendered into English above only a part of the verse 30.39. Retaining the rest of his rendering, this part would then read: 'And that which you give for profit so that it may increase in the wealth of the people, it does not increase with Allah.'

Here, in unmistakable terms, Allah Ta'ala specifies the kind of increase/profit that He abhors! He abhors - not all increases/profits, but - only that kind, which is sought to be made by unjustly usurping, during transactions, the wealth that should rightfully belong to other people. [As, for example, a factory owner, cutting down his expenses by paying less to his workers in order to make huge profits for himself on products, the workers help him manufacture.]

And it is this kind of *Riba* (increase/profit) that Allah Ta'ala mentions as *Ar-Riba* (the *Riba*)in verses, revealed later, and specifically prohibits in verse 2.275! How could the learned Judge, who is also a renowned Islamic scholar, could lose sight of this divine definition of the prohibited Riba **(Ar-Riba)** is beyond comprehension.

To make us understand better that it is the definition He is giving here, Allah Ta'ala, in His grace, has given us the similitude of *Zakaat* in this very verse. The literal meaning of zakaat is purity, but it is given the special meaning of 'charity' here and defined as that given to others purely for the pleasure of Allah. Just as riba is used in this verse without *Al*, so is *zakaat*. Just as *riba* is used in other verses with that Arabic definite article prefixed to it, so is *zakaat*. Therefore just as *Az-Zakaat* stands defined here, so is *Ar-Riba*.

And Allah Ta'ala, in His infinite mercy, further helps our understanding of this definition of *Ar-Riba* by juxta-positioning it with the contrasting definition of *Az-Zakaat*. While the latter involves the giving away our own wealth/property/dues to others, the former involves usurping unjustly, for our own use, the wealth/property/dues rightfully belonging to others.

It's a pity that most of us are blind to this so elaborately, variously and clearly given devine definition of *Ar-Riba*.

The existence of this divine definition, definitely precludes our acceptance of the narrow, unjust and man-given definition, even if the latter has now received the *fatwa* of acceptance from the Supreme Court of Pakistan. No Muslim can commit the unpardonable sin of *shirk*, by holding the Court - not equal to, but even - above, *nauzubillah*, Almighty Allah!

13. The second verse is of Surah Al-Nisaa where

the term *riba* is used in the context of sinful acts of the Jews in the following words:

وَأَخْذِهِمُ ٱلرِّبَوٰاْ وَقَدْ نُهُواْ عَنْهُ

"And because of their charging *riba* while they were prohibited from it." [An-Nisaa 4:161]

14. In the third verse of Surah Al-i-'Imran the prohibition of *riba* is laid down in the following words:

يَٰٓأَيُّهَا ٱلَّذِينَ ءَامَنُواْ لَا تَأْكُلُواْ ٱلرِّبَوٰٓاْ أَضْعَٰفًا مُّضَٰعَفَةً

"O those who believe do not eat up *riba* doubled and redoubled." [Al-i-'Imran 3:130]

15. The following set of verses is found in the Surah Al-Baqarah in the following words:

ٱلَّذِينَ يَأْكُلُونَ ٱلرِّبَوٰاْ لَا يَقُومُونَ إِلَّا كَمَا يَقُومُ ٱلَّذِى يَتَخَبَّطُهُ ٱلشَّيْطَٰنُ مِنَ ٱلْمَسِّ ذَٰلِكَ بِأَنَّهُمْ قَالُوٓاْ إِنَّمَا ٱلْبَيْعُ مِثْلُ ٱلرِّبَوٰاْ وَأَحَلَّ ٱللَّهُ ٱلْبَيْعَ وَحَرَّمَ ٱلرِّبَوٰاْ فَمَن جَآءَهُۥ مَوْعِظَةٌ مِّن رَّبِّهِۦ فَٱنتَهَىٰ فَلَهُۥ مَا سَلَفَ وَأَمْرُهُۥٓ إِلَى ٱللَّهِ وَمَنْ عَادَ فَأُوْلَٰٓئِكَ أَصْحَٰبُ ٱلنَّارِ هُمْ فِيهَا خَٰلِدُونَ ۝ يَمْحَقُ ٱللَّهُ ٱلرِّبَوٰاْ وَيُرْبِى ٱلصَّدَقَٰتِ وَٱللَّهُ لَا يُحِبُّ كُلَّ كَفَّارٍ أَثِيمٍ ۝ إِنَّ ٱلَّذِينَ ءَامَنُواْ وَعَمِلُواْ ٱلصَّٰلِحَٰتِ وَأَقَامُواْ ٱلصَّلَوٰةَ وَءَاتَوُاْ ٱلزَّكَوٰةَ لَهُمْ أَجْرُهُمْ عِندَ رَبِّهِمْ وَلَا خَوْفٌ عَلَيْهِمْ وَلَا هُمْ يَحْزَنُونَ ۝ يَٰٓأَيُّهَا ٱلَّذِينَ ءَامَنُواْ ٱتَّقُواْ ٱللَّهَ وَذَرُواْ مَا بَقِىَ مِنَ ٱلرِّبَوٰٓاْ إِن كُنتُم مُّؤْمِنِينَ ۝ فَإِن لَّمْ تَفْعَلُواْ فَأْذَنُواْ بِحَرْبٍ مِّنَ ٱللَّهِ وَرَسُولِهِۦ وَإِن تُبْتُمْ فَلَكُمْ رُءُوسُ أَمْوَٰلِكُمْ لَا تَظْلِمُونَ وَلَا تُظْلَمُونَ ۝ وَإِن كَانَ ذُو عُسْرَةٍ فَنَظِرَةٌ إِلَىٰ مَيْسَرَةٍ وَأَن تَصَدَّقُواْ خَيْرٌ لَّكُمْ إِن كُنتُمْ تَعْلَمُونَ ۝ وَٱتَّقُواْ يَوْمًا تُرْجَعُونَ فِيهِ إِلَى ٱللَّهِ ثُمَّ تُوَفَّىٰ كُلُّ نَفْسٍ مَّا كَسَبَتْ وَهُمْ لَا يُظْلَمُونَ ۝

"Those who take interest will not stand but as stands whom the demon has driven crazy by his touch. That is because they have said: 'Trading is but like *riba* '. And Allah has permitted trading and prohibited *riba* . So, whoever receives an advice from his Lord and stops, he is allowed what has passed, and his matter is up to Allah. And the ones who revert back, those are the people of Fire. There they remain for ever.

Allah destroys *riba* and nourishes charities. And Allah does not like any sinful disbeliever. Surely those who believe and do good deeds, establish Salah and pay Zakah, have their reward with their Lord, and there is no fear for them, nor shall they grieve.

O those who believe, fear Allah and give up what still remains of the *riba* if you are believers. But if you do not, then listen to the declaration of war from Allah and His Messenger. And if you repent, yours is your principal. Neither you wrong, nor be wronged. And if there be one in misery, then deferment till ease. And that you leave it as alms is far better for you, if you really know. And be fearful of a day when you shall be returned to Allah, then everybody shall be paid, in full, what he has earned. And they shall not be wronged." [Al-Baqarah 2:275-281]

Back to Top

Historical Analysis of the Verses of *Riba*

16. Before proceeding further it will be appropriate to understand these verses in their chronological order.

Surah Ar-Rum

17. First of these verses is a part of Surah Ar-Rum which was undisputedly revealed in Makkah. This verse is not of prohibitive nature. It simply says that the *riba* does not increase with Allah i.e. it carries no reward in the Hereafter. Many commentators of the Holy Qur'an are of the opinion that the word *riba* in this verse does not refer to usury or interest. Ibn Jarir Al-Tabari (D310 AH), the most famous exegete of the Holy Qur'an, reports from Ibn Abbas, Radi-Allahu anhu, and several Tabi'in like Saeed Ibn Jubair, Mujahid, Tawoos, Qatadah, Zahhak, and Ibrahim Al-Nakha'i that the word *riba* in this verse means a gift offered by someone to a person with the intention that the latter will give him in return a greater gift. However, some commentators of the Holy Qur'an have taken this word to mean usury. This view is attributed to Hasan Al-Basri as reported by Ibn Al-Jawzi. If the word *riba* used in this verse is taken to mean usury according to this view, which seems more probable, because the word of ' *riba* ' used in other places carries the same meaning, there is no specific prohibition against it in the verse. The most it has emphasized is that *riba*

does not carry a reward from Allah in the Hereafter. Therefore, this verse does not contain a prohibition against *riba* . However, it may be taken as a subtle indication to the fact that the practice is not favored by Allah.

My Comments : Please see my comments on paragraph 12 above.

Surah An-Nisaa

18. The second verse is of Surah al-Nisaa where, while listing the evil deeds of Jews, it is mentioned that they used to take *riba* which was prohibited for them. The exact time of this verse is very difficult to ascertain. The commentators are mostly silent on this point, but the context in which the verse was revealed suggests that it would have been revealed before the 4th year of Hijra. Verse 153 of the Surah Al-Nisaa is as follows:

يَسْـــَٔلُكَ أَهْـــلُ ٱلْكِــــتَٰبِ أَن تُـــنَزِّلَ عَلَيْهِـــمْ كِتَٰبًـــا مِّـــنَ ٱلسَّـــمَآءِ

> "The People of the Book ask you to bring down upon them a Book from the heaven." [An-Nisaa 4:153]

19. This verse implies that all the forthcoming verses were revealed in answer to the argumentation of the Jews who came to the Holy Prophet, Sall-Allahu alayhi wa sallam, and asked him to bring down a Book from the heavens like the one given to the Prophet Musa (Moses), alayhi salam. It means that this series of verses was revealed at a time when Jews were abundantly present in Madina and

were in a position to argue with the Holy Prophet, Sall-Allahu alayhi wa sallam. Since most of the Jews had left Madinah after 4th year from Hijra, this verse seems to have been revealed before that. Here the word *riba* undoubtedly refers to usury because it was really prohibited for the Jews. This prohibition is still contained in the Old Testament of the Bible. But it cannot be taken as a direct and explicit prohibition of *riba* for the Muslims. It simply mentions that *riba* was prohibited for the Jews but they did not comply with the prohibition in their practical lives. The inference, though, would be that it was a sinful act for the Muslims also, otherwise they had no occasion to blame the Jews for the practice.

My Comments 2: It is to be noted that while in verse 30.39, the word *riba* is used without the definite article *al,* in verse 4.161, it is used with the article prefixed to it. It is thus divinely indicated that *riba* (increase/gain/profit) mentioned here (verse 4.161) is the one already described/defined in a verse revealed earlier, i.e. in verse 30.39. Please see my detailed comments on paragraph 12 above.

Back to Top

Surah Al-i-'Imran

20. The third verse is of Surah Al-i-'Imran which is estimated to have been revealed sometime in the 2nd year after Hijra, because the context of the preceding and succeeding verses refers to the battle of Uhud which took place in the 2nd year after Hijra. This verse contains a clear prohibition for the

Muslims and it can safely be said that it is the first verse of the Holy Qur'an through which the practice of *riba* was forbidden for the Muslims in express terms. That is why Hafidh Ibn Hajar Al-Asqalani, the most famous commentator of Sahih Al-Bukhari, has opined that the prohibition of *riba* was declared sometime around the battle of Uhud. Some commentators have also pointed out the reason why this verse was revealed in the context of the battle of Uhud. They say that the invaders of Makkah had financed their army by taking usurious loans and had in this way arranged a lot of arms against Muslims. It was apprehended that it may induce the Muslims to arrange for arms on the same pattern by taking usurious loans from the people. In order to prevent them from this approach the verse was revealed containing a clear-cut prohibition of *riba* .

21. That the prohibition of *riba* had been imposed sometime around the battle of Uhud finds further support from an event reported by Abu Dawood in his As-Sunan from the noble companion, Abu Hurairah, Radi-Allahu anhu. The report says that Amr ibn Aqyash was a person who had advanced some loans on the basis of interest. He was inclined to embrace Islam but was reluctant to do so on the apprehension that after embracing Islam he would lose the amount of interest and therefore he delayed accepting Islam. In the meantime the battle of Uhud broke up whereby he decided not to delay embracing Islam and came to the battlefield, started fighting on behalf of Muslims and achieved the rank of a *Shaheed* (martyr) in the same battle.

22. This tradition clearly shows that *riba* was prohibited before the battle of Uhud and it was the

basic cause for the reluctance of Amr ibn Aqyash to embrace Islam.

<u>My Comments 3</u>: It is crystal clear from the wording of verse 3.130 that it (the verse) forbids Muslims from taking *Ar-Riba* <u>excessively</u> only. It may carefully be noted in this context that in verse 30.39, *Ar-Riba* was just abhorred, and not prohibited. And in verse 4.161, the believers were just informed how the Jews were and would be punished for their disobedience of the injunction imposed on them against *Ar-Riba*. The believers were, so to say, being mentally prepared for the injunction that was going to be imposed on the believers themselves! In verse 3.130, only excessive *Ar-Riba* was prohibited, and, finally, in verse 2.275, it was totally prohibited.

This was perfectly in keeping with the divine plan of eradicating a well-established evil practice - not at one stroke, but - step by step. The same plan of the Merciful Allah, was very much evident in the eradication of the evil of drinking wine.

It is therefore wrong on the part of the learned Judge to read into verse 3.130 anything other than its plain meaning, by relying on *ahaadheeth* that were recorded, in writing, <u>centuries</u> after the events.

23. The fourth set of verses is contained in Surah Al-Baqarah where the severity of the prohibition of *riba* has been elaborated in detail. The background

of the revelation of these verses is that after the conquest of Makkah, the Holy Prophet, Sall-Allahu alayhi wa sallam, had declared as void all the amounts of *riba* that were due at that time. The declaration embodied that nobody could claim anyinterest on any loan advanced by him. Then the Holy Prophet, Sall-Allahu alayhi wa sallam, proceeded to Taif which could not be conquered, but later on the inhabitants of Taif who belonged mostly to the tribe of Thaqif came to him and after embracing Islam surrendered to the Holy Prophet, Sall-Allahu alayhi wa sallam, and entered into a treaty with him. One of the proposed clauses of treaty was that Banu Thaqif will not forego the amounts of interest due on their debtors but their creditors will forego the amount of interest. The Holy Prophet, Sall-Allahu alayhi wa sallam, instead of signing that treaty simply wrote a sentence on the proposed draft that Banu Thaqif will have the same rights as the Muslims have. Banu Thaqif having the impression that their proposed treaty was accepted by the Holy Prophet, Sall-Allahu alayhi wa sallam, claimed the amount of interest from Banu Amr Ibn-al-Mughirah, but they declined to pay interest on the ground that *riba* was prohibited after Islam. The matter was placed before Attaab ibn Aseed, Radi-Allahu anhu, the governor of Makkah. Banu Thaqif argued that according to the treaty they are not bound to forego the amounts of interest. Attaab ibn Aseed, Radi-Allahu anhu, placed the matter before the Holy Prophet, Sall-Allahu alayhi wa sallam, on which the following verses of Surah Al-Baqarah were revealed:

يَٰٓأَيُّهَا ٱلَّذِينَ ءَامَنُواْ ٱتَّقُواْ ٱللَّهَ وَذَرُواْ مَا بَقِيَ مِنَ ٱلرِّبَوٰٓاْ إِن كُنتُم مُّؤْمِنِينَ ۝ فَإِن لَّمْ تَفْعَلُواْ فَأْذَنُواْ بِحَرْبٍ مِّنَ ٱللَّهِ وَرَسُولِهِۦۖ وَإِن تُبْتُمْ فَلَكُمْ رُءُوسُ أَمْوَٰلِكُمْ لَا تَظْلِمُونَ وَلَا تُظْلَمُونَ

"O those who believe, fear Allah and give up what still remains of the *riba* if you are believers. But if you do not, then listen to the declaration of war from Allah and His Messenger. And if you repent, yours is your principal. Neither you wrong, nor be wronged." [Al-Baqarah 2:278-279]

24. At that point of time Banu Thaqif surrendered and said we have no power to wage war against Allah and His Messenger.

<u>My Comments 4</u>: Please see the concluding part of my comments under paragraph 22 above, in this context also.

The Qur'aan was not revealed just for the people living at the time of its revelation. It was revealed for all the people living at all times till the Last Day. Therefore the scope of its verses cannot be restricted by the conditions prevailing at the time of revelation or by the circumstances under which those were revealed.

While describing those circumstances, the learned Judge makes the mistake of translating *Ar-Riba* occurring in the relevant *ahaadheeth* as 'interest' - even before he goes through the complete legal procedure of finding out what the Arabic term means. This was the very question placed before him for his decision. His final decision in the case therefore stands vitiated by this *faux pas*.

Back to Top

The Time of Prohibition of *Riba*

25. This study of the verses of the Holy Qur'an in the light of their historical background clearly proves that *riba* was prohibited at least in the 2nd year of Hijra. It is rather doubtful whether or not it was prohibited before that. If the word *riba* in the verses of Surah Ar-Rum is taken to mean usury as interpreted by a number of authorities, it would mean that the practice of *riba* was discarded by the Holy Qur'an in Makkan period. That is why a number of scholars are of the view that *riba* was never allowed in Islam. It was prohibited from the very beginning but the severity of prohibition was not emphasized during that period because Muslims were being persecuted by the infidels of Makkah and their major focus was on establishing and defending the basic articles of faith and they had no occasion to indulge in the practice of *riba*. Be that as it may, the fact that cannot be denied is that the express prohibition of *riba* was undoubtedly imposed in the 2nd year of Hijra.

26. Some appellants and juris-consults have assailed this statement and urged that the prohibition of *riba* was imposed in the last year of the life of the Holy Prophet, Sall-Allahu alayhi wa sallam. They tried to support this view on three different traditions:

27. Firstly, it has been reported in a number of traditions that the Holy Prophet, Sall-Allahu alayhi wa sallam, announced the prohibition of *riba* in his last sermon during his last Hajj. The Holy Prophet, Sall-Allahu alayhi wa sallam, not only prohibited *riba* on that occasion but had also declared that the first *riba* decreed to be void is the *riba* payable to his uncle Abbas ibn Abdul Muttalib, Radi-Allahu anhu. This declaration shows that the first transaction declared to be void was that of Abbas ibn Abdul Muttalib, Radi-Allahu anhu, which means that the prohibition of *riba* was not effective before the last Hajj of the Holy Prophet, Sall-Allahu alayhi wa sallam, i.e. before 10th year after Hijra.

28. A deeper study of the relevant material reveals that this argument is misconceived. In fact the prohibition of *riba* was effective at least from the 2nd year of Hijra but the Holy Prophet, Sall-Allahu alayhi wa sallam, deemed it necessary to announce the basic injunctions of Islam at the time of his last sermon which was the most attended gathering of his followers. To avail this opportunity, he announced the prohibition of a large number of practices prevalent in the days of Jahiliyya which were prohibited in Islam, but it did never mean that these practices were not prohibited before that point in time. For example, the Holy Prophet, Sall-Allahu alayhi wa sallam, has emphasized on the sanctity of human life and honor. He announced the prohibition of liquor and warned the Muslims against maltreatment of women, against back-biting and mutual quarrels. Obviously all these injunctions were effective since long ago, but the Holy Prophet, Sall-Allahu alayhi wa sallam, announced them at the time of his last sermon so that all the audience

may be fully aware of them and nobody could plead ignorance about these injunctions. The same is true about *riba* . It was prohibited long ago, but the announcement of its prohibition was repeated in express terms on that occasion also. At the same time the Holy Prophet, Sall-Allahu alayhi wa sallam, declared that no claim of *riba* will be entertained forthwith. It was a time when large number of Arab tribes were entering the fold of Islam throughout the peninsula. The practice of *riba* was rampant among them and it was apprehended that they would continue claiming the amounts of usury from one another, therefore, the Holy Prophet, Sall-Allahu alayhi wa sallam, deemed it fit to announce not only the prohibition of *riba* but also that all the previous transactions of *riba* will no more be honored. It was in this context that he declared the amounts of *riba* payable to his uncle Abbas ibn Abdul Muttalib, Radi-Allahu anhu, as void. It should be kept in mind that his uncle Abbas, Radi-Allahu anhu, embraced Islam in the 8th year after Hijrah shortly before the conquest of Makkah. Before embracing Islam he used to advance loans on the basis of interest and his debtors owed him huge amounts. It seems that after the conquest of Makkah he migrated to Madinah and could not settle his transactions with his debtors. Therefore, when he traveled for Hajj along with Holy Prophet, Sall-Allahu alayhi wa sallam, it was the first occasion when he could settle his transactions, hence, the Holy Prophet, Sall-Allahu alayhi wa sallam, declared that the whole amount of *riba* payable to his uncle Abbas, Radi-Allahu anhu, was void and no more payable. The words "first *riba* " occurring in this declaration do not mean that no *riba* was declared void before it. What it means is simply that this is the first amount of *riba* which is being declared as void at that occasion of the last sermon. We have already quoted the case of Banu Thaqif who demanded interest from their debtors after the conquest of Makkah (i.e. two years before the last Hajj) and the amounts of interest claimed by them were held to be void. It is therefore, not correct to say that the *riba* of Abbas bin Abdul Muttalib, Radi-Allahu anhu, was the first ever *riba* which was declared void, nor that the prohibition of *riba* was enforced for the first time at the time of the last Hajj.

My Comments 5: The question as to when exactly *Ar-Riba* was prohibited is only of academic interest for us now. Nor was this question raised before the court for its decision.

But it is unfortunate that the learned Judge, although being also renowned as an eminent Islamic scholar, should have relied, in this matter, on opinion that is clearly contrary to the indications given in the divine verses and even in the Traditions. Please also see my comments in this regard under paragraph 22 above.

Back to Top

The Last Verse of the Qur'an

29. Secondly, the view that *riba* was prohibited in the last days of the Holy Prophet, Sall-Allahu alayhi wa sallam, is sought to be supported by another tradition of Imam Bukhari where he has reported from Abdullah ibn Abbas, Radi-Allahu anhu, that he said:

آخر آية نزلت على النبي صلى الله عليه وسلم آية الربا

> "The last verse of the Holy Qur'an which was revealed on the Holy Prophet, Sall-Allahu alayhi wa sallam, was the verse of *riba*."

30. But in the first place Abdullah ibn Abbas, Radi-Allahu anhu, is not saying that the last injunction of Shar'iah was the prohibition of *riba*. All he is saying is that the last verse revealed on the Holy Prophet, Sall-Allahu alayhi wa sallam, was the verse of *riba* which in this sentence undoubtedly means the verse of Surah Al-Baqarah already quoted above. The words "verse of *riba* " is used as a title to it.

Therefore, even if the above statement of Abdullah ibn Abbas, Radi-Allahu anhu, is taken at its face value, it is an admission on his own part that the verses of Surah Al-i-'Imran, Surah An-Nisaa and Surah Ar-Rum were revealed before this verse of Surah Al-Baqarah, which clearly indicates that the prohibition of *riba* was already imposed before the revelation of these verses. It is, therefore, evident that this statement of Abdullah ibn Abbas, Radi-Allahu anhu, cannot be taken to mean that prohibition of *riba* was imposed in the last days of the life of the Holy Prophet, Sall-Allahu alayhi wa sallam.

31. Moreover, the same statement of Abdullah ibn Abbas, Radi-Allahu anhu, is reported by a number of other scholars, like Ibn Jarir Al-Tabari, who have explained that this statement of Abdullah ibn

Abbas, Radi-Allahu anhu, refers only to the following verse:

$$\text{وَاتَّقُوا يَوْمًا تُرْجَعُونَ فِيهِ إِلَى اللَّهِ ثُمَّ تُوَفَّىٰ كُلُّ نَفْسٍ مَّا كَسَبَتْ وَهُمْ لَا يُظْلَمُونَ}$$

> "And be fearful of a day when you shall be returned to Allah, then everybody shall be paid, in full, what he has earned. And they shall not be wronged." [Al-Baqarah 2:281]

32. Since this verse is placed in the present order immediately after the verses of *riba* which are 275-280, Abdullah ibn Abbas Radi-Allahu anhu, has termed it as a verse of *riba*. That is why Imam Bukhari has related this statement of Abdullah ibn Abbas, Radi-Allahu anhu, in that chapter of his Kitab-al-Tafseer which deals with the commentary on verse 281 only and not in the chapters 49-52 which deal with verses 275-280. In the light of this explanation, it is more probable that according to Abdullah ibn Abbas, Radi-Allahu anhu, the verses mentioning the severity of the prohibition of *riba* (verses 275-280 of Surah Al-Baqarah) were already revealed and it was only verse 281 which was revealed in the last days of the Holy Prophet, Sall-Allahu alayhi wa sallam. This view finds further support from the fact that verse 278 was certainly revealed soon after the conquest of Makkah when the tribe of Thaqif had claimed the amount of *riba* outstanding toward Banu Mughira as already mentioned in detail. The conquest of Makkah was in the 8th year of Hijra while the Holy Prophet, Sall-Allahu alayhi wa sallam, passed away in the 11th year of Hijra. How can it be imagined that no

other verse of Holy Qur'an was revealed during this long period of more than 3 years. This presumption which is false on the face of it is very difficult to be attributed to a person like Abdullah ibn Abbas, Radi-Allahu anhu. It is, therefore, almost certain that by the verse of *riba* he did not mean any verse other than verse 281 which according to him was revealed separately in the last days of the Holy Prophet, Sall-Allahu alayhi wa sallam, and this too is the personal opinion of Abdullah ibn Abbas, Radi-Allahu anhu. Some other Sahabah have identified some other verses of the Holy Qur'an as being the last revealed verses. The issue has been discussed in detail by Al-Suyyuti in his Al-Itqan and many other books of Tafseer and Hadith.

33. This explanation is more than sufficient to prove that the prohibition of *riba* was imposed long before the last days of the Holy Prophet, Sall-Allahu alayhi wa sallam.

34. The upshot of the above discussion is that although some indications of displeasure against *riba* were given in the Makkan period also, but the express prohibition of *riba* was revealed in the Holy Qur'an sometime around the battle of Uhud in the second year of Hijra.

35. The third tradition relied upon by some appellants for their claim that the prohibition of *riba* came in the last days of the Holy Prophet, Sall-Allahu alayhi wa sallam, is a statement of Sayyidna Umar, Radi-Allahu anhu. We shall analyze this statement later on in para 56 in greater detail insha-Allah.

My Comments: Please see my comments under paragraph 28 above.

Back to Top

What is Meant by *Riba*?

36. Now we come to the question what is meant by *riba* ? The Holy Qur'an did not give any definition for the term for the simple reason that it was well known to its immediate audience. It is like the prohibition of pork, liquor, gambling, adultery etc, which were imposed without giving any hard and fast definition because all these terms were well known and there was no ambiguity in their meaning. Similar was the case of *riba*. It was not a term foreign to Arabs. They all used the term in their mutual transactions. Not only Arabs but all the previous societies used to practice it in their financial dealings and nobody had any confusion about its exact sense. We have already quoted the verse of Surah An-Nisaa where the Holy Qur'an has reproached the Jews for their taking *riba* while it was prohibited for them. Here this practice is termed as *riba* in the same manner as it is termed in Surah Al-i-'Imran or Surah Al-Baqarah. It means that the practice of *riba* prohibited for Muslims was the same as was prohibited for the Jews.

My Comments 6: Please see my detailed comments in this regard under paragraphs 12, 19, 22 and 24 above. There has been no controversy at all as regards the meanings of the Arabic words for pork, liquor, gambling and adultery. Therefore there was no need for giving any special definitions for these words.

But that is not the case with *riba*. As already stated in my comments herein above, this Arabic word literally means increase/growth/gain/profit. Obviously, Allah Ta'ala has not prohibited every imaginable kind of increase etc. It ought to be only a particular kind that is prohibited. There was therefore a crying need to define which kind. Verse 30.39 does just that. It is therefore unfortunate for the eminent Islamic scholar to hold that the 'Holy Qur'an did not give any definition for the term.' As the divine Book elsewhere remarks, "Look, how they invent a lie against Allah ..." [Q: 4.50]

Back to Top

Riba in the Bible

37. This prohibition is still available in the Old Testament of the Bible. The following excerpts may be quoted with advantage:

> "Thou shalt not lend upon usury to thy brother; usury of money, usury of victuals, usury of anything that is lent upon usury." [Deuteronomy 23:19]

> "Lord, who shall abide in thy tabernacle? Who shall dwell in thy holy hill? He that walketh uprightly, and worketh righteousness and speaketh the truth in his heart. He that putteth not out of his money to

usury, nor taketh reward against the innocent." [Psalms 15:1, 2, 5]

"He that by usury and unjust gain increaseth his substance, he shall gather it for him that will pity the poor." [Proverbs 28:8]

"Then I consulted with myself, and I rebuked the nobles, and rules and said unto them, Ye exact usury, every one of his brother. And I set a great assembly against them." [Nehemiah 5:7]

"He that hath not given forth upon usury, neither hath taken any increase, that hath withdrawn his hand from iniguity, hath executed true judgment between man and man, hath walked in my statues, and hath kept my judgments, to deal truly; he is just. He shall surely live, said the Lord God." [Ezekiel 18:8.9]

"In thee have they taken gifts to shed blood; thou hast taken usury and increase, and though hast greedily gained of thy neighbors by extortion, and hast forgotten me, said the Lord God." [Ezekiel 22:12]

38. In these excerpts of the Bible the word usury is used in the sense of any amount claimed by the creditor over and above the principal advanced by him to the debtor. The word *riba* used in the Holy

Qur'an carries the same meaning because the verse of Surah An-Nisaa explicitly mentions that *riba* was prohibited for the Jews also.

My Comments 7: Usury is interest taken at exorbitant or illegal rates. Such interest does fit in the Qur'aanic definition of *Ar-Riba* as given in verse 30.39. The learned Judge's attempt at treating usury as synonymous with interest is unwarranted.

Back to Top

The Definition of *Riba* as given by the Exegetes of the Holy Qur'an

39. Moreover, the literature of Hadith while explaining the word *riba* has mentioned in detail the transactions of *riba* which were used to be effected by the Arabs of Jahiliyya on the basis of which the earliest commentators of the Holy Qur'an have defined *riba* in clear terms.

40. Imam Abubakr Al-Jassas (D.380 AH) in his famous work Ahkamul Qur'an has explained *riba* in the following words:

والربا الذى كانت العرب تعرفه وتفعله إنما كان قرض الدراهم والدنانير إلى اجل بزيادة على مقدار ما استقرض على مايتراضون به

> "And the *riba* which was known to and practiced by the Arabs was that they used to advance loan in the form of Dirham (silver coin) or Dinar (gold coin) for a certain term

with an agreed increase on the amount of the principal advanced."

41. On the basis of this practice the same author has defined the term in the following words:

هو القرض المشروط فيه الأجل وزيادة مال على المستقرض

"The *riba* of Jahiliyya is a loan given for stipulated period with a stipulated increase on the principal payable by the loanee."

42. The well-known Imam Fakhruddin Al-Raazi has mentioned the practice of *riba* in the days of Jahiliyya as follows:

وأما ربا النسيئة فهو الأمر الذى كان مشهورا متعارفا فى الجاهلية وذلك أنهم كانوا يدفعون المال على أن يأخذوا كل شهر قدرا معينا، ويكون رأس المال باقيا، ثم إذا حل الدين طالبوا المديون برأس المال، فإن تعذر عليه الأداء زادوا فى الحق والأجل، فهذا هو الربا الذى كانوا فى الجاهلية يتعاملون به.

"As for the *riba An-Nasiah*, it was a transaction well-known and recognized in the days of Jahiliyya i.e. they used to give money with a condition that they will charge a particular amount monthly and the principal will remain due as it is. Then on the maturity date they demanded the debtor to pay the principal. If he could not pay, they would increase the term and the payable amount. So it was the *riba* practiced by the people of Jahiliyya."

The same explanation is given by Aadil Al-Dimashqi in his detailed Tafseer Al-Lubaab v.4 p.448.

Back to Top

The Detailed Account of *Riba al-Jahiliyya*

43. Mr. Riazul Hassan Gillani, the learned counsel for the Federation of Pakistan argued before us that *riba al-Jahiliyya* which was prohibited by the Holy Qur'an was a particular transaction in which no increase used to be stipulated at the time of advancing a loan; however, if the debtor could not pay the principal amount at the time of maturity, the creditor used to offer him two options: either to pay the principal or to increase the amount in exchange of an additional term allowed by the creditor. The learned counsel argued that the original loan advanced in the days of Jahiliyya would not stipulate any additional amount in the principal, and therefore, any amount stipulated in the original contract of loan does not fall within the definition of *riba* al-Qur'an. However, it may fall in the definition of *riba -al-Fadl* which is a Makruh (detested, not advisable) practice.

44. The learned counsel referred to a number of traditions narrated by the exegetes of the Holy Qur'an. For example, he cited the well-known Tafseer of Ibn Jarrir At-Tabari who on the authority of Mujahid has explained the *riba* of Jahiliyya as follows:

كانوا فى الجاهلية يكون للرجل على الرجل الدين، فيقول: لك كذا وكذا وتؤخر عنى.

"In the days of Jahiliyya a person used to owe a debt to his creditor then he would say to his creditor, 'I offer you such and such amount and you give me more time to pay.'"

45. The same explanation has been given by a number of commentators of the Holy Qur'an. Mr. Riazul Hassan Gillani argued that there is no mention in these traditions of any increase on the principal stipulated in the original transaction of loan. What is mentioned here is that the increase used to be offered or claimed at the time of maturity which shows that *riba* prohibited by the Holy Qur'an was restricted to claiming an amount for giving an additional time to the debtor. If an increased amount is stipulated in the initial transaction of loan, it is not covered by *riba al-Qur'an*.

46. This contention of the learned counsel did not appeal to us at all, for the simple reason that a careful study of the relevant material in the original resources of Tafseer clearly shows that the claim of an increased amount over the principal had different forms in the days of Jahiliyya. Firstly, while advancing a loan the creditor used to claim an increased amount over the principal and would advance loan on this clearly stipulated condition as is mentioned by Imam Al-Jassas in his Ahkamul Qur'an already quoted above. Secondly, the creditor used to charge a monthly return from the debtor while the principal amount would remain intact up to the day of maturity as mentioned by Imam Ar-Raazi and Ibn Aadil already quoted.

47. The third form is mentioned by Mujahid as quoted by the learned counsel, but the full explanation of this transaction is given by Ibn Jarir himself on the authority of Qatadah in the following words:

عن قتادة أن ربا الجاهلية بيع الرجل البيع إلى أجل مسمى فإذا حل الأجل ولم يكن عند صاحبه قضاء زاده أخر عنه

> "The *Riba* of Jahiliyya was a transaction whereby a person used to sell a commodity for a price payable at a future specific date, thereafter when the date of payment came and the buyer was not able to pay, the seller used to increase the amount due and give him more time."

48. The same explanation has been given by al-Suyuti on the authority of Faryabi in the following words:

كانوا يتبايعون إلى الأجل، فإذا حل الأجل زادوا عليهم وزادوا في الأجل.

> "They used to purchase a commodity on the basis of deferred payment, then on the date of maturity the sellers used to increase the due amount and increase the time of payment."

49. It is clear from these quotations that the transaction in which the creditor used to charge an additional amount on the date of maturity was not a transaction of loan. Initially; it used to be a

transaction of sale of a commodity on deferred payment basis in which the seller used to fix a higher price because of deferred payment, but when the buyer would not pay at the date of maturity, the seller used to keep on increasing the amount in exchange of additional time given to the buyer. This particular transaction is meant by Mujahid also, that is why, he did not use the word Qarz (loan); he has rather used the word Dain (debt) which is normally created by a transaction of sale.

50 . This form of *Riba* has been frequently mentioned by the commentators of the Holy Qur'an because they wanted to explain a particular sentence of the verses of *Riba* which is as follows:

$$\text{قَالُوٓاْ إِنَّمَا ٱلۡبَيۡعُ مِثۡلُ ٱلرِّبَوٰٓاْ}$$

"The non-believers say that sale is very similar to Riba." [Al-Baqarah 2:275]

51. This saying of the non-believers clearly refers to the particular transaction of sale mentioned above. Their objection was that when we increase the price of commodity in the original transaction of sale because of its being based on deferred payment, it is treated as a valid sale. But when we want to increase the due amount after the maturity date, when the debtor is not able to pay, it is termed as *Riba* while the increase in both cases seems to be similar. This objection of the non-believers of Makkah has been specifically mentioned by the famous commentator Ibn Abi Hatim on the authority of Said ibn Jubair:

قالوا: سواء علينا إن زدنا فى أول البيع، أو عند محل المال فهما سواء فذلك
قوله: قالوا أنما البيع مثل الربوا.

> "They used to say that it is all equal whether we increase the price in the beginning of the sale, or we increase it at the time of maturity. Both are equal. It is this objection which has been referred to in the verse by saying 'They say that the sale is very similar to *Riba*.'"

52. The same explanation is given in al-Bahr al-Muheet by Abu Hayyan and several other original commentators of the Holy Qur'an.

53. It clearly shows that the practice of increase at the time of maturity relates to two situations: firstly, a situation where the original transaction was that of sale of a commodity as mentioned by Qatadah, Faryabi, Saeed Ibn Jubair etc, and the second situation was where the original transaction was that of a loan whereby monthly interest used to be charged by the creditor and the principal amount used to remain intact until the date of maturity, and if the debtor would not pay the principal at that point of time, the creditor used to increase the due amount on the principal in exchange of further time given to debtor as mentioned by Imam Raazi and Ibn Aadil etc already quoted in paras 42 and 43 above.

54. It is thus established that the *Riba* prohibited by the Holy Qur'an was not confined to the transaction referred to by Mr. Riazul Hassan Gillani, the learned counsel for the Federation of Pakistan. It

had different forms which all were practiced by the Arabs of Jahiliyya. The common feature of all these transactions is that an increased amount was charged on the principal amount of a debt. At times, this debt was created through a transaction of sale and it was created through a loan. Similarly, the increased amount was at times charged on monthly basis, while the principal was to be paid at a stipulated date, and some time it was charged along with the principal. All these forms used to be called *Riba* because the lexical meaning of the term is *increase* . That is why, the commentators of the Holy Qur'an like Imam Abubakr al-Jassas have defined the term in the following words:

هو القرض المشروط فيه الأجل و زيادة مال على المستقرض

"The *Riba* of Jahiliyya is a loan given for a stipulated period against increase on the principal payable by the Loanee."

My Comments 8: Readers may please note how, without divine guidance, creatures would have a free-for-all. As can be seen from the foregoing paragraphs of the Judgement, a number of definitions for *Ar-Riba* were put forth by different scholars, on the assumption that the Qur'aan has not defined the term. And then, fourteen centuries after Allah Ta'ala declared in the Qur'aan that He had perfected the Religion of Islam (see verse 5.3), a Court of His creatures sits in judgement and confirms that indeed, the Qur'aan has not defined the term! It then proceeds to give its own *fatwa* as to what *Ar-Riba* should really mean. It rules that besides *riba-al-Qur'aan* there are three other categories to be together known as *riba-al-Sunnah!*

But that does not bring us to the end of the controversy. Who knows, Supreme Courts of other Islamic countries, in future, may as well give us some other definitions of the Qur'aanic term!

The scenario that thus presents itself is far from being stable, clear or unambiguous. How can a divinely guaranteed perfect Religion present such an uncertain picture of an injunction, which it imposes on its followers!? How can the followers abide by the injunction unless they, exactly and without any ambiguity, know what it means!? And how can there be absolute certainty about the meaning unless it is divinely given!?

The unfortunate, bitter and unpalatable fact of the matter is that the Honourable Judge has unwittingly blasphemed Islam by holding that the Qur'aan has not defned the Arabic term 'Ar-Riba'.

It stands very much defined in verse 30.39 and its meaning further explained and elaborated in the other *Ar-Riba* verses. The learned Judge's statement, moreover, is expressly contrary to the oft-repeated Qur'aanic assertion that its verses are clearly and variously explained in details for people to understand.

And in view of the existence of the Qur'aanic definition of *Ar-Riba,* the entire proceedings of this court case has been an exercise in futility.

55. Now we come to the different arguments advanced before us against the prohibition of the modern interest.

Back to Top

The Statement of Sayyidna Umar, Radi-Allahu anhu, About the Ambiguity in the Concept of *Riba*

56. Mr. Abu Bakr Chundrigar, the learned counsel for Habib Bank Ltd. placed his reliance on an article written by Mr. Justice (late) Qadeeruddin Ahmad, which appeared in daily DAWN dated 12 August 1994. In this article the late Justice Qadeeruddin Ahmad contended that the term *Riba* as used in the Holy Qur'an is an ambiguous term, correct meaning of which was not understood even by some companions of the Holy Prophet, Sall-Allahu alayhi wa sallam. He referred to the statement of Sayyidna Umar, Radi-Allahu anhu, that the verses of *Riba* were among the "last verses of the Holy Qur'an and the Holy Prophet, Sall-Allahu alayhi wa sallam, passed away before he could explain them to us, therefore, avoid *Riba* and every thing which is doubtful." The same argument has been adopted by a number of appellants in their memos of appeal so much so that some of the appellants have termed the verses of *Riba* as *Mutashabihaat* (the verses having ambiguity or confusion in their meaning). They argued that the Holy Qur'an has asked us to follow only those verses which are clear in meaning (

Muhkamaat) and not to follow *Mutashabihaat* . The verses of *Riba* being of the second category, according to the appellants, they are not practicable.

57. This argument is fallacious on the face of it, because in the verse of Surah al-Baqarah Allah almighty declared war against those who do not avoid the practice of *Riba* . How could one imagine that Allah Almighty, the All-Wise, the All-Merciful, can wage war against a practice, the correct nature of which is not known to anybody.

In fact the term *Mutashabihaat* used in the beginning of Surah Al-i-'Imran of the Holy Qur'an refers to two kinds of verses: firstly, they refer to some words used in the beginning of different Surahs, the correct meaning of which is not known to any body for sure, like, "Alif Lam Mim Ra", but the ignorance of the correct meaning of these words does not affect the lives of Muslims because no precept of Shar'iah has been given through these words. Secondly, the word *Mutashabihaat* refers to some attributes of Almighty Allah, the exact nature of which is not conceivable by a human being. For example, Holy Qur'an has referred to the 'hand of Allah' in certain places (like An-Nisaa 3:73, Al-Maidah 5:63, Al-Fat-h 48:10). No body knows what is the nature of the hand of Allah, nor is it necessary for one to know, because no practical issue depends on its knowledge, but some people used to indulge in the quest of their exact nature which was neither their responsibility to discover nor did any practical precept of Shar'iah depend on their understanding. Allah Almighty has forbidden those people from indulging in the hypothetical discussion about the nature of these attributes because it had no concern with the practical precepts of Shar'iah they were required to follow. But it never happened that a practical rule of Shar'iah is termed as *Mutashabihaat*. It is not only declared by the Holy Qur'an (in Al-Baqarah 2:233) but it is also a matter of common sense that Allah never burdens a people with a command the obedience of which is beyond their control/ability. If the correct meaning of *Riba* was not known to any body, Almighty Allah could not have made it incumbent on the Muslims to avoid it. A plain reading of the verses of Surah al-Baqarah reveals that *Riba* has been declared a very grave sin and its gravity is emphasized in an unparalleled manner when it was said that if the Muslims did not leave this practice, they should face a declaration of war from Allah and His Messenger.

My Comments 9: I feel sad to note that, despite the learned Judge's correct analysis of *Ar-Riba* verses being not among the *Mutashabihaat* and despite his recognition, made earlier, of the fact that the lexical meaning of *riba* is 'increase', he failed to see the crying need of a divine definition for *Ar-Riba*. I do indeed feel sad to note that he failed to see this definition clearly given in verse 30.39.

Back to Top

A Description of *Riba al-Fadl*

58. So far as the statement of Sayyidna Umar, Radi-Allahu anhu, is concerned, it will be necessary before analyzing it to note that the Holy Qur'an had prohibited the *Riba* of Jahiliyya with all their forms

already mentioned above. All these forms related to the transactions of a loan or a debt created by sale etc. But after the revelations of these verses, the Holy Prophet, Sall-Allahu alayhi wa sallam, prohibited some other transactions as well, which were not known previously as *Riba* . The Holy Prophet, Sall-Allahu alayhi wa sallam, felt that, given the commercial atmosphere at that time, certain barter transactions might lead the people to indulge in *Riba*. The Arabs used certain commodities like wheat, barley, dates etc., as a medium of exchange to purchase other things. The Holy Prophet, Sall-Allahu alayhi wa sallam, treating these commodities as a medium of exchange like money, issued the following injunction:

والذهب بالذهب، والفضة بالفضة، والبر بالبر، والشعير بالشعير والتمر بالتمر، والملح بالملح، مثلا بمثل، يدا بيدا، فمن زاد أو استزاد فقد أربى.

> "Gold for gold, silver for silver, wheat for wheat, barley for barley, date for date, salt for salt, must be equal on both sides and hand to hand. Whoever pays more or demands more (on either side) indulges in *Riba*."

59. It means that if wheat is exchanged for wheat, the quantity on both sides must be equal to each other and if the quantity of any one side is more or less than the other, this transaction is also a *Riba* transaction, because in the tribal system of Arab these commodities were used as money, and the exchange of one kilogram of wheat for one and a half (1 1/2) kilogram of another wheat would stand for the exchange of one dirham for one and a half (1

1/2) dirham. However, this transaction was termed as *riba* by the Holy Prophet, Sall-Allahu alayhi wa sallam, and this meaning was not covered by the term '*riba al-Jahiliyya*'. Therefore, it was called as '*riba al-fadl*' or '*riba-al-sunnah*'.

60. It is to be noted that, while prohibiting the *riba al-fadl*, the Holy Prophet, Sall-Allahu alayhi wa sallam, has identified only six commodities and it was not clearly mentioned in the above hadith whether this rule is limited to these six commodities or it is applicable to some other commodities as well, and in the latter case what are those commodities? This question raised controversy among the Muslim jurists. Some earlier jurists, like Qatadah and Tawoos, restricted this rule to these six commodities only, while the other jurists were of the opinion that the rule will be extended to other commodities of the same nature. Then there was a difference of opinion about the nature of these commodities that might be taken as a common feature found in all the six commodities and a criterion for identifying the commodities which are subject to the same rule. Imam Abu Hanifa and Imam Ahmad are of the opinion that the common feature of these six commodities is that they can either be weighed or measured, therefore, any commodity which is sold by weighing or measuring falls within this category and is subject to the same rule, if it is bartered with a similar commodity. Imam al-Shafii is of the view that the common feature of these six commodities is that they are either eatables or they are used as a universal legal tender. Wheat, barley, date, salt represent eatables while gold and silver represent universal legal tenders. Therefore, according to Imam al-Shafii all

eatables and universal legal tenders are subject to the rule mentioned in the hadith. Imam Malik is of the opinion that the common feature among these six commodities is that they are either food items or they can be stored. Therefore he holds that every thing that is a food item or can be stored is included in the same category, hence, subject to the same rule.

61. This difference of opinion among the Muslim jurists was based on the fact that after specifying the six commodities the Holy Prophet, Sall-Allahu alayhi wa sallam, did not expressly mention whether or not other commodities will assume the same status.

Back to Top

The Correct Meaning of Sayyidna Umar's Statement

62. It is in this background that Sayyidna Umar, Radi-Allahu anhu, has stated that the Holy Prophet, Sall-Allahu alayhi wa sallam, passed away before giving any specific direction with regard to this difference of opinion. A deeper study of the statement of Sayyidna Umar, Radi-Allahu anhu, reveals that he was doubtful only about the *Riba al-fadl* mentioned in the hadith cited above, and not about the original *Riba* which was prohibited by the Holy Qur'an and was practiced by the Arabs of Jahiliyya in their transactions of loan and non-barter sales. This is evident from the most authentic version of the statement of Sayyidna Umar, Radi-Allahu anhu, reported in the Sahih of al-Bukhari

and Muslim. The words reported by Bukhari are as follows:

ثلاث وددت أن رسول الله صلى الله عليه وسلم لم يفارقنا حتى يعهد إلينا عهدا: الجد، والكلالة، وأبواب من أبواب الربا.

"There are three things about which I wished that the Holy Prophet, Sall-Allahu alayhi wa sallam, did not leave us before explaining them to us in detail: the inheritance of grand father and the inheritance of Kalalah (a person who has left neither a father nor a son) and some issues relating to *Riba* ."

63. Moreover, at another occasion Sayyidna Umar, Radi-Allahu anhu, has clarified his position in the following words:

إنكم تزعمون أنا لا نعلم أبواب الربا، ولأن أكون أعلمها أحب إلي من أن يكون لي مصر و كورها، ومن الأمور أمور لايكن يخفين على أحد هو: أن يباع الذهب بالورق نسيئا.

"You think that we do not know about any issue from the issues of *Riba* - and no doubt I would love to know all these issues' more than I would like to own a country like Egypt with all its habitations - but there are many issues (about *Riba*) which cannot be unknown to any one e.g. purchasing gold for silver on deferred payment basis."

64. These narrations of the statement of Sayyidna Umar, Radi-Allahu anhu, clearly reveal two points: firstly, that all his concern in the issues of *Riba* related to *Riba al-Fadl* and not to *Riba al-Nasiah* which was prohibited by the Holy Qur'an, and secondly, that even in the issue of *Riba al-Fadl* he did not feel difficulty in many transactions which were clearly prohibited, however, he was doubtful only with regard to some transactions which were not expressly mentioned in the relevant Hadith or in any other saying of the Holy Prophet, Sall-Allahu alayhi wa sallam.

65. An objection may be raised on the above explanation. According to a narration reported by Ibn Majah, Sayyidna Umar, Radi-Allahu anhu, had declared that the verse of *Riba* was the last revealed verse of the Holy Qur'an, therefore, the Holy Prophet, Sall-Allahu alayhi wa sallam, passed away before explaining it in full terms.' This narration shows that the doubts of Sayyidna Umar, Radi-Allahu anhu, related to the same *Riba* as was prohibited by the Holy Qur'an and not to *Riba al-Fadl* . But after studying different sources narrating this statement of Sayyidna Umar, Radi-Allahu anhu, it transpires that the narration of Ibn Majah is not as authentic as that of Bukhari and Muslim. One of the narrators in the report of Ibn Majah is Saeed Ibn Abi Arubah who has been held by the experts of Hadith as a person who used to confuse one narration with the other. We have already quoted the exact words reported by Bukhari and Muslim with very authentic chain of narrators. None of them has attributed to Sayyidna Umar, Radi-Allahu anhu, that the verse of *Riba* was the last verse of the Holy Qur'an. It seems that a narrator like Saeed Ibn

Abi Arubah has confused the exact words of Sayyidna Umar, Radi-Allahu anhu, with the words of Sayyidna Ibn Abbas, Radi-Allahu anhu, already discussed or with his own view that the verse of *Riba* was the last verse of the Holy Qur'an. We have already explained in detail the real facts in this respect and that it was not correct to believe that *Riba* was prohibited in the last days of the Holy Prophet, Sall-Allahu alayhi wa sallam, or that the verses of *Riba* were the last revealed verses of the Holy Qur'an. Therefore, the version given by Ibn Majah cannot be relied upon while correctly assessing the statement of Sayyidna Umar, Radi-Allahu anhu. It is consequently established that whatever doubts Sayyidna Umar, Radi-Allahu anhu, had in his mind about *Riba* were relevant to *Riba al-Fadl* only. So far as *Riba al-Qur'an* or *Riba al-Nasiah* is concerned, he had not the slightest doubt about its nature and its prohibition.

<u>My Comments 10</u>: The foregoing paragraphs provide ample proof that if *ahaadeeth* on *Ar-Riba* are read on the assumption that the Qur'aan has not provided any definition for this term *(Ar-Riba)*, one is likely to be led into a web of controversies. Such controversies, in turn, would lead to doubts on Islam being a perfect Religion. But such doubts are absurd in view of the divine assertion (verse 5.3) that Islam is a perfect Religion.

Applying the principle of *reductio ad absurdum,* therefore, the assumption - that the Qur'aan has not provided the definition - has got to be <u>wrong</u>!

The *hadeeth* attributed to Caliph Umar, in the

illuminating light of verse 5.3, could only mean that the *Sunnah* does not give the full explanation on *Ar-Riba,* but that the Qur'aan does! For further details of my analysis on this Tradition, please refer Chapter VII of my Book *ISLAM & INTEREST*. The Book also gives an explanation of the 'Gold for gold etc.' *hadeeth* quoted in paragraph 58 above, in the illuminating light of verse 30.39.

Back to Top

Productive or Consumption Loans

66. Another argument advanced by some appellants was that the Holy Qur'an had prohibited to claim any increase over and above the principal in the case of consumption loans only, where the borrowers used to be poor person's borrowing money to meet their day to day needs of food and clothes etc. Since no productive loans were in vogue in the days of Holy Prophet, Sall-Allahu alayhi wa sallam, it was not contemplated by the verse of *Riba* to prohibit a charge on the commercial and productive loans. Otherwise also, they argued, it is injustice to claim any additional amount on the principal from a poor person, but it is not so in the case of a rich man who borrows money to develop his own commercial enterprise and earn huge profits through it. Therefore, it is only the loans of the first kind i.e. consumption loans on which any excess is termed as *Riba* and not an increased amount charged on the commercial loans.

67. We have paid due consideration to this argument but it could not stand the academic scrutiny for three reasons:

Back to Top

(i) Validity of a Transaction is not Based on the Financial Status of a Party

68. Firstly, the validity of a financial or commercial transaction does never depend on the financial position of the parties. It rather depends on the intrinsic nature of the transaction itself. If a transaction is valid by its nature, it is valid irrespective of whether the parties are rich or poor. Sale, for example, is a valid transaction whereby a lawful profit is generated. It is allowed regardless of whether the purchaser is rich or poor. Lease is a lawful transaction and it is permissible even though the lessee is a poor person. The most one can say is that a poor purchaser or a poor lessee deserves concession on humanitarian grounds, but one cannot say that charging any amount of profit from him is totally haram or prohibited. If a poor person wants to purchase bread from a baker, one can say that the baker should not charge a high profit from him, but no one can say that the baker is obligated to sell the bread to him at his cost and any profit charged by him above the cost is totally unlawful for which he deserves hell. If a poor person hires a taxi, one can advise the owner of the taxi to give some concession to him on the basis of his poverty, but no one can reasonably assert that the owner of the taxi must not charge any fare from him or must not charge a fare higher than his actual expense, otherwise his income will be held as haram and

analogous to waging war against Allah and His Messenger. The baker has opened his shop to earn a lawful profit through the transaction of sale which is intrinsically a valid transaction, and he deserves a reasonable profit for his investment and labor, even though the purchaser is poor. If he is obligated to sell his breads to all the poor persons at his cost price, he can neither run his shop nor can earn livelihood for his children. Similarly, the one who runs a taxi for rendering transport services to the passengers is allowed to charge a reasonable fare from those benefiting from his service. If he is required to render this service to all poor persons free of charge, he cannot run the taxi. Nobody has, therefore, ever claimed that charging any profit or a fee or a fare from a poor person is totally haram. The reason is that profit, fee and fare, being lawful charges deserved by valid transactions, may be charged from the persons benefiting from the commodities sold or services rendered, even though the benefiting persons are poor.

69. On the other hand, the prohibited transactions are invalidated on the basis of their intrinsic nature and not on the basis of the financial position of the parties. Gambling is prohibited for both rich and poor persons. Bribery is unlawful regardless of whether the bribe is charged from the rich or from the poor. It is, therefore, evident that it is not the richness or poverty of the parties that renders a transaction valid or invalid. It is the intrinsic nature of the transaction that really determines its validity or otherwise.

70. The case of charging interest from a debtor is in no way different. If it is a valid charge according to

its intrinsic nature, it should be allowed, even though the debtor is poor, but if it is an invalid charge by itself, it should be unlawful irrespective of the financial position of the parties. There is no justification for distinguishing the case of interest from that of a sale in this respect by restricting the former's validity to the rich borrowers only while charging of profit in a sale is allowed from both rich and poor persons. In fact, the notion that interest is prohibited only where the borrower is poor is totally against the well-established principles of business and trade where the validity of transactions is judged on the basis of their own strength and not on the identity of the parties involved.

71. Moreover, 'poverty' is a relative term which has different degrees. Once it is accepted that interest cannot be charged from the poor, while it is quite lawful to be charged from the rich, who will have the authority to determine the exact degree of poverty required for exempting a person from the charge of interest? If the distinction between lawful and unlawful interest is drawn on the basis of the purpose of the loan, and the loans taken for consumption are exempted from the charge of interest, as urged by some appellants, the consumption itself may be of different kinds which range from food items to luxurious objects. Even if the 'consumption' is restricted to the requirements of one's life, they too vary from person to person. One may argue that private transport has become one of the necessities of life and therefore he is entitled to take an interest-free loan for purchasing a car. House is one of the fundamental necessities of one's life and no interest can be charged on millions of rupees borrowed for the purpose of constructing or

purchasing a house, because all these borrowings fall within the category of 'consumption loans'. On the other hand, if an unemployed person borrows a few hundred rupees to start hawking on the streets, it will be quite lawful to charge interest from him, because his loan does not fall within the definition of a 'consumption loan'.

72. It is thus clear that the permissibility of interest can neither be based on the financial position of the debtor, nor on the purpose for which money is borrowed, and therefore the distinction between consumption loans and productive loans in this respect is contrary to the well-established principles.

Back to Top

(ii) **The Nature of Qur'anic Prohibitions**

73. The. second reason for which this argument is not tenable, is that the verses which prohibit *riba* do not at all differentiate between a consumption or a commercial loan, nor does this difference find any mention whatsoever in the vast literature of the Sunnah dealing with *riba* . Even if it is presumed for the sake of argument that commercial loans were not in vogue in the days of the Holy Prophet, Sall-Allahu alayhi wa sallam, it does not justify the insertion of a new condition in the concept of *riba* which, as established earlier, was quite clear in the minds of the addressees of the Holy Qur'an. The Holy Qur'an has prohibited *riba* in general terms which includes all the forms of *riba* whether prevalent at the time of its revelation or not. When the Holy Qur'an prohibits a transaction, it is not a

particular form of the transaction that is meant by the prohibition. It is the basic concept of the transaction which is hit by the injunction. When liquor was prohibited, it was not only the particular forms of liquor available in those days which were forbidden, it was the substance of liquor which was banned, and nobody can reasonably claim that the new forms of liquor which were not available in the days of the Holy Prophet, Sall-Allahu alayhi wa sallam, are not hit by the prohibition. When *qimar* (gambling) was declared as haram the purpose was not to restrict the prohibition only to those forms of gambling which were in vogue at that time. The prohibition, in fact, encompassed all its present and future forms, and no one can sensibly argue that the modern forms of gambling are not covered by the prohibition. We have already discussed the meaning of the term *riba* as understood by the Arabs and as interpreted by the Holy Prophet, Sall-Allahu alayhi wa sallam, and his noble companions, and that it covered any stipulated additional amount over the principal in a transaction of loan or debt. This concept had many forms in the days of the Holy Prophet, Sall-Allahu alayhi wa sallam, may have taken other forms in the later ages and still may take some other forms in future, but as long as the said basic feature of the transaction remains intact, it will certainly invoke the prohibition.

Back to Top

(iii) **Banking and Productive Loans in the Age of Antiquity**

74. Thirdly, it is not correct to say that commercial or productive loans were not in vogue when *riba*

was prohibited. More than enough material has now come on the record to prove that commercial and productive loans were not foreign to the Arabs, and that loans were advanced for productive purposes both before and after the advent of Islam.

75. In fact the academic and historical research has discovered the fallacy of the impression that mercantile loans and banking transactions are the invention of the 17th century CE. Modern discoveries have shown that the history of banking transactions refers back to a period not less than two thousand years before Christ. The Encyclopaedia Britannica, while discussing the history of banks, has detailed the early traces of the banking transactions. The relevant article begins with the following remark:

> "Pastoral nations such as Hebrews, while they maintained money-lenders, had no system of banks that would be considered adequate from the modern point of view. But as early as 2000 BC, the Babylonians had developed such a system. It was not the result of private initiate, as that time, but an incidental service performed by the organized and wealthy institution of the cult. The temples of Babylon, like those of Egypt, were also the banks. "The shekels of silver" runs a Babylonian document, "have been borrowed by Mas-Schamach, the son of Adadrimeni, from the Sun-priestess Amat-Schamach, daughter of Warad-

Enlil. He will pay the Sun-God's interest. At the time of the harvest he will pay back the sum and the interest upon it." It is evident enough that the priestess Amat-Schamach was merely the accredited agent of the institution . No doubt the clay tablet with the inscription corresponds to what we call negotiable commercial paper. Another document of the same period was certainly such. It runs: "Warad-Ilisch, the son of Taribum, has received from the Sun-Priestess Iltani, daughter of Ibbatum, one shekel silver by the sun-God's balance. This sum is to be used to buy sesame. At the time of the sesame-harvest, he will repay in sesame, at the current price, to the bearer of this document."

76. The article has then detailed how the banking operations developed from religious institutions to private business institutions, until in 575 BC there was a banking institution in Babylon, the Igibi bank of Babylon. The records of this bank show that it acted as buying agent for clients; loaned on crops, attaching them in advance to ensure reimbursement; loaned on signatures and on objects deposited and received deposits on interest. The article has further detailed that similar banking institutions existed also in Greece, Rome, Egypt, etc. centuries before Christ and they deposited money, lent it on interest and extensively used letters of credit, financial papers and traded in them.

77. Will Durant, the famous historian, has given a detailed account of the banking transactions prevalent in Greece in the fifth century before Christ. He has mentioned that despite interest being denounced even by the philosophers, there were banks in Greece:

> "Some deposit their money in temple treasuries. The temples serve as banks, and lend to individuals and states at a moderate interest; the temple of Apollo at Delphi is in some measure an international bank for all Greece. There are no private loans to governments, but occasionally one state lends to another. Meanwhile the money-changer at his table (trapeza) begins in the fifth century to receive money on deposit, and to lend it to merchants at interest rates that vary from 12 to 30 percent according to the risk; in this way he becomes a banker, though to the end of ancient Greece he keeps his early name of trapezite, the man at the table. He takes his methods from the near East, improves them, and passes them on to Rome, which hands them down to modern Europe. Soon after the Persian War, Themistocles deposits seventy talents ($420,000) with the Corinthian banker Philostephanus, very much as political adventurers feather foreign nests for themselves today; this is the earliest known

allusion to secular-nontemple-banking. Towards the end of the century Antisthenes and Archestrtus establish what will become, under Pasion, the most famous of all private Greek banks. Through such trapezitai money circulates more freely and rapidly, and so does more work, than before, and the facilities that they offer stimulate creatively the expansion of Athenian trade."

78. Even in the days closer to the advent of Islam in Arabia, all kinds of commercial, industrial and agricultural loans advanced on the basis of interest were prevalent in the Byzantine Empire ruling in Syria, to the extent that Justinian, the Byzantine emperor (527-565 A.D) had to promulgate a law determining the rates of interest which could be charged from different types of borrowers. Gibbon has detailed the contents of the Code of Justinian and that it allowed the rate of 4% charged as interest from illustrious people, 6% charged from general people as ordinary rate of interest, 8% from the manufacturers and merchants and 12% from nautical insurers. The exact words of Gibbon are as follows:

> "Persons of illustrious rank were confined to the moderate profit of Four Per Cent; six was pronounced to be the ordinary and legal standard of interest; eight was allowed for the convenience of manufacturers and merchants; twelve was granted to nautical insurers."

79. The underlined part of the above passage shows that the practice of commercial loans was so widespread in the Roman Empire that a separate law was enforced to fix their rate of interest. This law of Justinian was promulgated in Byzantine Empire shortly before the birth of the Holy Prophet, Sall-Allahu alayhi wa sallam, in Arabia (Justinian died in 565 CE while the Holy Prophet, Sall-Allahu alayhi wa sallam, was born in 570 CE) and obviously the law remained in force for quite a long time after its promulgation. On the other hand the Arabs, especially of Makkah, had constant business relations with Syria, one of the most civilized provinces of the Byzantine Empire. As we shall see later in detail, the Arabs trade caravans used to export goods to and import other goods from Syria. Their economic and financial relations with the Byzantine Empire were so prominent that the currency used throughout the Arabian peninsula was the dirhams (of silver) and dinars (of gold) coined by the Byzantine Empire, so much so that the poets have referred to the Dinars as Ceazarians. Kuthair 'Uzzah, of the famous Arab poets says:

يروق عيون الناظرات كأنه هرقلي وزن أحمر التبر راجح

80. Ibn-al-Anbari quotes another poet saying:

دنانير مما شيف في ارض قيصر

81. Rather, some contemporary writers have claimed that the nomenclature of the Arabic coins (dirham, diner and fals) is originally derived from the Greece or latin words which are very similar to these names. These Byzantine coins remained in use

throughout the Muslim world till the year 76 A.H., when Abdulmalik ibn Marwan started coining his own dinars.

82. Keeping in view such close financial relations of the Arabs with the Roman Empire, how can it be imagined that the Arabs were totally unaware of the credit transactions flourishing in the Roman Empire? As we shall see later, the business-relations of the Arabs were not restricted to Syria. They extended to Iraq, Egypt, and Ethiopia as well. They were fully aware of the business style of these countries, and their awareness about the interest based transactions of these countries is reflected in an advice given by Abdullah b. Salaam, Radi-Allahu anhu, (a native of Madinah) to Abu Burdah (who had settled in Iraq and came to visit Madinah). Abdullah b. Salaam, Radi-Allahu anhu, warned him that he was living in a country where *riba* had wide currency, and therefore, he should be very careful while dealing with other people lest he should indulge in *riba* unconsciously. The same advice was given by Sayyidna Ubayy ibn Kab, Radi-Allahu anhu, to his pupil Zirr b. Hubaish.

Back to Top

Commercial Interest in Arabia

83. Coming to the case of Arabian peninsula itself, no one can deny the fact that trade was the most outstanding economic activity of the Arabs. Makkah, in particular, consisted of barren lands and hills with very little amount of water and therefore was totally unfit for cultivation. That is why commerce and trade was the basic characteristic of

the economic life of the Arabs of Makkah. One of the most outstanding features of the Arabian trade was that their commercial activities were not restricted to their own land. Their main business was to export their own goods to all the surrounding countries and import their goods to their own cities. For this purpose their commercial caravans used to travel to Syria, Iraq, Egypt, Ethiopia etc. The history of these trade-caravans refers back to a period as early as that of the holy Prophet Yaqoob, alayhi salam, (Jacob or Israel). It is mentioned by the Holy Qur'an that the brothers of Sayyidna Yousuf, alayhi salam, (Joseph) had thrown him in a pit from where a passing caravan picked up and sold him in Egypt. According to historical evidence, this caravan was an Arab caravan consisting of the children of Ismail, alayhi salam, who had embarked on a business tour to export goods to Egypt. This fact finds mention in the Old Testament of the Bible itself which says:

> "And they sat down to eat bread: and they lifted up their eyes and looked, and, behold, a company of Ishmaelites came from Gilad with their camels bearing spicery and balm and myrrh, going to carry it down to Egypt." [Genesis 37:25]

84. This Arab caravan was going to export spices, balms, and perfumes in such an early period to such a distant country, Egypt, that was thousands of miles away from the center of Arabia. It may show the extent to which the Arabs had deployed their courageous entrepreneurship right from the beginning of their history.

85. Naturally, the commercial activities of the Arabs kept on increasing in the later days, so much so that they were identified as a trading nation. How far their international trade had flourished before the advent of Islam has been detailed by the historians, and it is neither possible nor necessary to give all these details here, but the fact that the Arabs were trade-oriented people can hardly be questioned by a person who has studied their history. The importance of their trade caravans can be assessed by the fact that the Holy Qur'an has revealed a full Surah (Al-Qureish) to denote that their business towards Yemen in winter and towards Syria in summer were a blessing from Allah on account of their services to Kabah. The Holy Qur'an has specifically mentioned the term ilaaf which refers to the commercial treaties the Arabs of Quraish had with different nations and tribes. The size of these caravans may be imagined from the fact that the caravan led by Abu Sufyan at the time of the battle of Badr consisted of one thousand camels and had returned with 100% profit (one dinar for every one dinar).

86. Obviously, the caravan of this huge size could not be owned by any one individual. It was a collective enterprise of the whole tribe and was funded by the contributions of all the members of the tribe like a joint stock company. The historians have noted that:

لم يبق قرشى ولا قرشية له مثقال إلا بعث به فى العير

"There remained no male or female in the tribe of Quraish who had one misqaal of gold and had not contributed to the caravan."

87. It was not only the caravan of Abu Sufyan that was funded in this manner. Almost all the big caravans used to be organized on the same pattern.

88. Keeping this commercial atmosphere in view, one can hardly imagine that the Arabs were not familiar with commercial loans, or that their loans were restricted to consumption purposes. But apart from hypothesis, there are concrete evidences that they used to borrow money for their commercial and productive needs. Some of these evidences are summarized below.

(a) Dr. Jawed Ali, whose extensive research about the Arabs of jahiliyyah is appreciated throughout the academic world, has analyzed the funding sources of these caravans and has remarked as under:

ويظهر مما ذكره أهل الأخبار وأو ردوه عن قوافل مكة أن مال القافلة لم يكن مال رجل واحد، أو أسرة معينة بل كان يخص تجارا من أسر مختلفة، وأفرادا وجد عندهم المال، أو اقتر ضوه من غيرهم فرموه فى رأس مال القافلة أملا فى ربح كبير.

"What the historians have narrated about the caravans of Makkah reveals that the capital of a caravan never used to be the capital of one individual or a particular family; it rather belonged to the traders of different families and to those individuals who themselves had money or had borrowed it from

> others and had contributed it to the capital of the caravan, with a hope to earn huge profit."

The underlined sentence shows that these caravans used to be funded, inter alia, by the commercial loans.

(b) All the books of tafseer have mentioned the background of the verses of Surah al-Baqarah dealing with *riba* . Almost all of them have reported that different tribes of Arabia used to take interest-based loans from each other. For example, Ibn Jarir al-Tabari says:

> كانت بنو عمر و بن عمير بن عوف يأخذون الربا من بنى المغيرة'
> وكانت بنو المغيرة يربون لهم فى الجاهلية

> "The tribe of Banu Amr used to charge interest from the tribe of Banu al-Mughirah and Banu al-Mughirah used to pay them interest."

These loans were not taken by one individual from another. Instead, the tribe as a collective entity used to borrow money from another tribe. We have already shown that the tribes of Arabia used to work as a joint stock company for the purpose of funding their trade-caravans and in order to undertake their joint enterprise. Therefore, the loans taken by one tribe from the other were not for the purpose of consumption only; they were certainly commercial loans meant to finance their commercial ventures.

(c) While explaining the verse of Surah Al-Rum (30:39), already quoted in Para No. 17 of this judgment, Ibn Jarir al-Tabari has reported the view of some earlier commentators of the Holy Qur'an that this verse refers to the practice of some people in jahilliyah who would finance some others to increase the wealth of the recipients. Ibn Jarir has supported this view by the following statement of Sayyidna Ibn Abbas, Radi-Allahu anhu.

ألم تر إلى الرجل يقول للرجل: لأمولنك فيعطيه، فهذا لا يربوا عندالله لأنه يعطيه لغير الله يرى به ماله

> "Have you not seen a person saying to another, 'I shall certainly finance you' then he gives him? So, this does not increase with Allah, because he gives him not to please Allah, but to increase his wealth."

He has also quoted the following statement of Ibrahim al-Nakhai in the same context:

كان هذا فى الجاهلية يعطى أحدهم ذا القرابة المال يكثر به ماله

> "It was in the days of jahiliyyah that one used to give money to one of his relatives to increase his wealth."

Obviously, financing for the purpose of increasing wealth of the recipient means that the recipient would invest this money to earn profit and thereby increase his wealth. These statements of Ibn Abbas, Radi-Allahu anhu, and Ibrahim al-Nakhai clearly show that the practice of financing for productive purposes was so prevalent in the Arab Society that, according to these commentators, the verse of Surah al-Rum was revealed in that context.

(d) The concept of commercial loan finds mention in a hadith of the Holy Prophet, Sall-Allahu alayhi wa sallam, himself, which is reported by Imam Ahmad, Al-Bazzar and Al-Tabarani from Abdurrahman ibn Abi Bakr, Radi-Allahu anhu. According to him, the Holy Prophet, Sall-Allahu alayhi wa sallam, has said:

> "Allah Almighty will call a debtor on the Day of Judgment. He will stand before Allah and will be asked O son of Adam, why did you take this loan and why did you violate the rights of the people? He will say, My Lord, you know that I have taken this loan, but neither used it in a eating or drinking nor in wearing clothes nor in doing something, instead, I was afflicted either by fire or by theft or by a business loss. Allah will say, My slave has told the truth. I am the best One who will pay today on your behalf."

The underlined words contemplate that this person had borrowed money for commercial purpose whereafter he suffered a business loss. It shows that the concept of the loans taken for commercial purposes was quite clear even in the mind of the Holy Prophet, Sall-Allahu alayhi wa sallam.

(e) The Holy Prophet, Sall-Allahu alayhi wa sallam, has, in another authentic hadith reported by Imam Bukhari, narrated the story of an Israelite person who had borrowed one thousand dinars from another person and then embarked on a sea voyage.

Some other reports have expressly mentioned that this borrowing was for commercial purpose. Moreover, such a huge amount cannot be borrowed for normal consumption needs, and the hadith mentions that the borrower set out on his sea voyage and after the date of maturity he earned so much that he sent one thousand dinars to his creditor, and offered to pay him the same amount once more under the impression that the first payment did not reach him, but the creditor admitted that he had received the amount and therefore he refused the debtor's offer to pay him once more.

There is another example of where the Holy Prophet, Sall-Allahu alayhi wa sallam, himself has referred to a commercial loan.

(f) Apart from the practice of the trade-caravans detailed above, there are many examples to show that the commercial loans used to be given and taken on individual level as well. Some of the examples are given below:

> (i) Abu Lahab, the uncle off the Holy Prophet, Sall-Allahu alayhi wa sallam, was one of the most inimical persons towards him, but he did not participate personally in the battle of Badr. The reason was that he had advanced a loan of four thousand dirhams on interest to one Asi bin Hisham and when he could not repay it, he hired his debtor against his loan to replace him in the battle. Obviously, this amount of four

thousand dirhams was too big (in those days) to be borrowed by a starving person to satisfy his hunger. It was certainly borrowed for the purpose of trade which could not bring fruit and the debtor stood bankrupt.

(ii) It is reported by several books of hadith and history that Sayyidna Zubair Ibn Awwam, Radi-Allahu anhu, was one of the richest companions of the Holy Prophet, Sall-Allahu alayhi wa sallam. On account of his credibility people wanted to deposit their money with him in trust, but he refused to receive any deposit from any one unless he gives it to him as a loan. It was beneficial for the depositor, because after treating it as a loan, Sayyidna Zubair, Radi-Allahu anhu, was liable to repay it in any case, while in the case of a simple deposit in trust, he would not be liable to repay if the amount is lost by theft, fire etc. Once the people deposited money with Sayyidna Zubair, Radi-Allahu anhu, as a loan, he invested the money in trade. The manner in which Sayyidna Zubair, Radi-Allahu anhu, used to receive deposits and invest them in trade is very similar to a private bank. It is reported by Imam Bukhari that his liabilities toward his depositors were calculated, at the time of his death, to be two million and two hundred thousand, and all this amount was invested in commercial projects.

(iii) Ibn Saad has reported Sayyidna Umar, Radi-Allahu anhu, wanted to send a trade caravan to Sriya, and for that purpose he borrowed four thousand dirhams from Sayyidna Abdurrahman ibn Awaf, Radi-Allahu anhu.

(iv) Ibn Jarrir has reported that Hind, daughter of Utbah and wife of Abu Sufyan borrowed four thousand dirhams from Sayyidna Umar, Radi-Allahu anhu, for the purpose of her trade. She invested this money in purchasing goods and selling them in the market of the tribe of Kalb.

(v) Al-Baihaqi has reported that Sayyidna Miqdad ibn Aswad, Radi-Allahu anhu, borrowed seven thousand dirhams from Sayyidna Usman, Radi-Allahu anhu. Obviously, this amount was not borrowed by a poor person for his consumption needs, because Sayyidna Miqdad, Radi-Allahu anhu, the borrower, was of the rich Sahabah who was the only one riding a horse in the battle of Badr and whose agricultural produce was purchased by Sayyidna Muawiyah,

Radi-Allahu anhu, for 100,000/- dirhams.

(vi) When Sayyidna Umar, Radi-Allahu anhu, received the fatal blow from a Christian, he called his son and directed him to calculate the amounts he owed to his creditors. His son calculated the amount and found that it was 80,000 dirhams. Some people advised Sayyidna Umar, Radi-Allahu anhu, to borrow this money from Baitulmal, so that he may relieve himself from his liability towards the people and that the debt of the Baitulmal might be settled after selling his assets, but Sayyidna Umar, Radi-Allahu anhu, rejected the suggestion and directed his sons to pay the amount from his own assets. Obviously, this amount of 80,000 dirhams could not have been borrowed for personal consumption.

(vii) Imam Maalik has reported in his Al-Muwatta that Abdullah and Ubaidullah, the two sons of Sayyidna Umar, Radi-Allahu anhu, went to Iraq for the purpose of Jihad. While coming back they met Abu Musa Al-Ashari, Radi-Allahu anhu, the governor of the City of Basra. He told them he wanted to send some money of the public exchequer to Sayyidna Umar, Radi-Allahu anhu, in Madina. Instead of giving them that money in trust, he suggested that he give it to them as a loan so that it may remain in the risk of Abdullah and Ubaidullah and may reach safely to Sayyidna Umar, Radi-Allahu anhu, and it was beneficial for Abdullah and Ubaidullah as well because after taking the amount as loan, they could purchase some goods from Iraq and sell them in Madina and after settling the principal amount to Sayyidna Umar, Radi-Allahu anhu, they could earn some profit. They accepted the suggestion and acted accordingly. When after reaching Madina they paid the principal amount to Sayyidna Umar, Radi-Allahu anhu, he asked them whether Abu Musa, Radi-Allahu anhu, had given such a loan to all the members of the army as well. They replied in negative. Sayyidna Umar, Radi-Allahu anhu, said, "He has given you this loan only because of your relationship with me, therefore, you will have to return not only the principal but also the profit earned through it." Ubaidullah Ibn Umar objected that this decision was not just, because if the goods purchased by them were destroyed in the way, they would have born the risk and were liable to pay the principal amount in any case, therefore, they deserve the profit they earned. Still Sayyidna Umar, Radi-Allahu anhu, insisted to return the profit to Baitulmal. One of the persons present at that time suggested to Sayyidna Umar, Radi-Allahu anhu, that instead of claiming all the profit from them, he might convert this transaction into Mudarabah through which half of the profit would be deserved by Abdullah and Ubaidullah and the remaining half would go to Baitulmaal. Sayyidna Umar, Radi-Allahu anhu, accepted this proposal and acted accordingly. Obviously the loan advanced to Abdullah and Obaidullah in this case was a commercial loan contemplated from the very beginning to be invested in trade.

89. The above material is more than enough to prove that the concept of commercial loans was not alien to the Holy Prophet, Sall-Allahu alayhi wa sallam, or his companions when *riba* was prohibited. Therefore, it is not correct to say that the prohibition of *riba* was restricted to the consumption loans only and it did not refer to the commercial loans.

<u>My Comments 11</u>: The point that no distinction can be made between consumption loans and commercial loans in the matter of *Ar-Riba,* is well argued by the learned Judge. There can, indeed, be no distinction. The kind of the loan cannot be

made the determining factor for the purpose of covering it under *Ar-Riba*.

But the educative and informative analysis of the learned Judge has been of no avail, because he failed to see the divine purpose of verse 30.39. He has sought to interpret the verse in the light of *ahaadheeth*, which purport to give the background and the circumstances in which the verse was revealed.

As already mentioned herein above in my comments, the Qur'aan was not revealed just for the people living at the time of its revelation. It was revealed for all the peoples living at all the times till the Last Day. It is extremely unfortunate that eminent scholars even, have lost sight of this important fact. They have consequently tended to deviate from the plain meaning of the divine verses as in the case of verse 30.39.

My detailed comments under paragraph 12 above may please be perused in this context.

Back to Top

Excessive Rates of Interest

90. Another argument advanced on behalf of some appellants was that the prohibition of *riba* is applicable only to those interest transactions where the rate of interest is exorbitant or excessive. This argument is sought to be supported by the verse of Surah Al-i-'Imran:

يَـٰٓأَيُّهَا ٱلَّذِينَ ءَامَنُوا۟ لَا تَأْكُلُوا۟ ٱلرِّبَوٰٓا۟ أَضْعَـٰفًا مُّضَـٰعَفَةً ۖ وَٱتَّقُوا۟ ٱللَّهَ لَعَلَّكُمْ تُفْلِحُونَ ۝

> "O ye who believe! devour not Usury, doubled and multiplied; but fear Allah; that ye may (really) prosper." [Al-i-'Imran 3:130]

91. It is argued that this verse of the Holy Qur'an is the first verse that came with a clear prohibition of *riba*, but it has qualified the prohibition by the words "doubled and multiplied" to denote that the practice of *riba* is forbidden only when the rate is so excessive that it makes the payable amount twice that of the principal. The logical result of this expression would be that if the rate of interest is not so high, the prohibition is not applicable. The interest charged in the present banking system, it is argued, is not normally so high as to make the payable amount double the principal, and, therefore, the banking interest is not covered by the prohibition.

92. This argument overlooks the fact that the different verses of the Holy Qur'an relating to the same subject must be studied in juxtaposition with each other. No verse can be interpreted in isolation from the other relevant material available in other parts of the Holy Qur'an. As explained at the very beginning, the Holy Qur'an has dealt with the subject of *riba* in four different chapters. Obviously, no verse can contradict another verse on the same subject. The most detailed treatment of the subject of *riba* is found in Surah Al-Baqarah, the relevant verses of which have already been quoted and

translated in paragraph 15 of this judgment. These verses include the following command:

$$\text{يَٰأَيُّهَا ٱلَّذِينَ ءَامَنُوا۟ ٱتَّقُوا۟ ٱللَّهَ وَذَرُوا۟ مَا بَقِىَ مِنَ ٱلرِّبَوٰٓا۟ إِن كُنتُم مُّؤْمِنِينَ}$$

> "O those who believe fear Allah and give up whatever remains of *riba*, if you are believers." [Al-Baqarah 2:278]

93. The words "whatever remains of *riba*" in this verse indicate that every amount over and above the principal has to be given up. This point is further clarified in express terms by the following sentence:

$$\text{وَإِن تُبْتُمْ فَلَكُمْ رُءُوسُ أَمْوَٰلِكُمْ}$$

> "And if you repent (from the practice of *riba*) then you are entitled to get back your principal."

94. These words do not leave any ambiguity in the fact that repentance from the practice of *riba* is not possible unless any amount exceeding the principal is given up and that a lender is entitled only to the principal he has actually advanced. A combined study of the verses of Surah Al-i-'Imran and Surah Al-Baqarah leaves no doubt that the words "doubled and multiplied" occurring in Surah Al-i-'Imran are not of restrictive nature, and that "doubled and multiplied" is not a necessary condition for the prohibition of *riba*. These words have rather been

used to refer to the worst kind of practice of *riba* rampant at that time.

95. In order to fully understand the point, we must refer to one of the basic principles of the interpretation of the Holy Qur'an. The Holy Book is not originally a statute book meant to be used as a legal text. It is a book of guidance which, along with certain laws or commandments, embodies many expressions having persuasive value. Unlike the text of a statute book, the Holy Qur'an contains some words or expressions used either for emphasis or for explaining the evil results of a particular act. They are not meant to be taken as a restrictive qualification for the command or the prohibition preceding them. A self-evident example of this style of the Holy Qur'an is the verse which says:

"Do not sell my verses for a little price." [Al-Baqarah 2:41]

96. Nobody can take this verse to mean that selling the verses of the Holy Qur'an is prohibited only because the price claimed is very low and that if the verses are sold for a higher price, the practice can be held as permissible. Every person of common sense can easily understand that the words "for a little price" used in this verse are not of restrictive nature. They are rather meant to indicate the evil practice of some people who used to commit the grave sin of selling the verses of the Holy Qur'an and still did not gain much in financial terms. It never means that the blame is directed towards the

"little price" they gain; rather the blame is directed to the selling of verses itself.

97. Similarly, at another place the Holy Qur'an says:

وَلَا تُكْرِهُواْ فَتَيَاتِكُمْ عَلَى ٱلْبِغَآءِ إِنْ أَرَدْنَ تَحَصُّنًا

> "And do not force your slave girls to prostitution if they want to remain chaste." [An-Nur 24:33]

98. Obviously it does not mean that if the girls do not want to remain chaste, one can force them to prostitution. What the verse means is that although the prostitution in itself is a grave sin, yet it becomes all the more evil if a girl is forced to indulge in this profession while she intends to remain chaste. The words "if they want to remain chaste" are not of restrictive nature meant to qualify the prohibition with their desire to remain chaste. These words have been added only to indicate the increased severity of the crime. It is in the same style that the words "doubled or redoubled" have been used with *riba* in the verse of Surah Al-i-'Imran. They are not intended to qualify the prohibition of *riba* with doubling or redoubling. They are only meant to emphasize the added severity of the sin if the interest charged is so exorbitant or excessive. This intention of the verse of the Holy Qur'an is quite evident in the light of the verse of Surah Al-Baqarah already quoted above.

99. Secondly, the interpretation of the Holy Qur'an should always be based on the explanation given by or inferred from the Ahadith of the Holy Prophet,

Sall-Allahu alayhi wa sallam, and his noble companions who were the direct recipients of the revelation and were fully familiar with the context of the verse and the environment in which it was revealed. From this aspect as well, it is certain that the prohibition of *riba* was never meant to be restricted to a particular rate of interest. The prohibition was meant to cover every amount charged in excess of the principal, however small it may be. The following Ahadith are sufficient to prove this point:

(i) We have already mentioned that the Holy Prophet, Sall-Allahu alayhi wa sallam, made a general declaration of the prohibition of *riba* at the time of his last sermon on the occasion of his last Hajj. The words used by him in that sermon, as reported by Ibn Abi Hatim, were as follows:

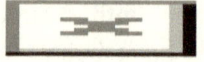

(The original text image was missing in the original source itself)

"Listen, every amount of interest that was due in Jahiliyya is now declared void for you in its entirety. You are entitled only to your principal whereby neither you wrong nor be wronged. And the first liability of interest declared to be void is the interest of Abbas ibn Abd-ul-Muttalib which is hereby declared void in its entirety."

Here the Holy Prophet, Sall-Allahu alayhi wa sallam, declared the total amount exceeding the principal as nullified in its entirety. He has left no ambiguity in the fact that the creditors will be entitled to get back only the principal and will not be able to charge even a penny over and above the principal amount.

(ii) It is reported by Hammad b, Salamah in his Jame from Sayyidna Abu Hurairah, Radi-Allahu anhu, that the Holy Prophet, Sall-Allahu alayhi wa sallam, has said:

إذا ارتهن شاة شرب المرتهن من لبنها بقدر علفها فإن استفضل من اللبن بعد ثمن العلف فهو ربا.

"If the creditor received a goat as mortgage from the debtor, the creditor may use its milk to the extent he has spent in providing fodder to the goat. However, if the milk is more than the price of the fodder, the excess is *riba*."

(iii) Imam Maalik has reported the following ruling of Abdullah Ibn Umar, Radi-Allahu anhu:

من اسلف سلفا فلا يشترط إلا قضاؤه

"Whoever advances a loan must not stipulate except that the principal loan shall be repayable."

(iv) Imam Maalik has also narrated in the same chapter that Abdullah Ibn Masood, Radi-Allahu anhu, used to say.

من أسلف سلفا فلا يشترط أفضل منه وإن كان قبضة من علف فهو ربا

"Whoever advances a loan cannot stipulate in the agreement that he will receive something better than he has advanced. Even if it be a handful of fodder, it is *riba*."

(v) It is reported by Imam Al-Baihaqi that a person said to Abdullah Ibn Masood, Radi-Allahu anhu:

"I have taken a loan of 500 from a person on a condition that I shall lend him my horse for riding.

Abdullah Ibn Masood, Radi-Allahu anhu, answered:

"Whatever benefit of riding your creditor will receive, it will be *riba*."

(vi) The same author has reported that Sayyidna Anas Ibn Maalik, Radi-Allahu anhu, was asked about a person who advances a loan to someone and then the debtor gives him something as a gift, will it be permissible for him to accept that gift? Sayyidna Anas Ibn Maalik, Radi-Allahu anhu answered that the Holy Prophet, Sall-Allahu alayhi wa sallam, has said:

إذا اقرض أحدكم قرضا فأهدى إليه طبقا فلا يقبله، أو حمله على دابة، فلا يركبها إلا أن يكون بينه وبينه قبل ذلك

"If one of you has advanced a loan and the debtor offer the creditor a bowl (of food), he should not accept it, or if the debtor offers him a ride of his animal (cattle) the debtor must not take the ride unless this type of gift has been a usual practice between them before advancing the loan".

The substance of the hadith is that if the debtor and creditor were on friendly terms with each other and it was their habit that one of them used to give a gift to the other, then this type of gift can be acceptable even after the recipient has advanced a loan to the giver. However, if there were no such terms between the creditor and the debtor before the loan transaction, then the debtor should not accept it, because it will have smell of *riba*.

(vii) The same author, Al-Baihaqi, has reported from Abdullah Ibn Abbas, Radi-Allahu anhu, who was asked about a person who owed 20 Dirhams to another person, and started offering his creditor some gifts. Whenever the creditor received a gift, he sold it in the market until the aggregate amount received by the creditor reached 13 dirhams. Abdullah Ibn Abbas, Radi-Allahu anhu, advised the creditor not to take more than 7 dirhams.

(viii) It is reported by Sayyidna Ali, Radi-Allahu anhu, that the Holy Prophet, Sall-Allahu alayhi wa sallam, has said,

كل قرض جر منفعة فهو ربا

> "Every loan that derives a benefit (to the creditor) is *riba*."

This hadith is reported by Harith ibn Abi Usamah in his Musnad.

100. Mr. Riazul Hasan Gilani, the learned counsel for the Federation of Pakistan assailed the authenticity of this hadith on the ground that certain scholars of hadith have taken it as a weak hadith. He referred to Allamah Munawi who has held its chain of narrators as weak.

101. It is true that certain critics of the hadith have not accepted this tradition as authentic, because one of its narrators, Sawwar b. Musab, is held to be unreliable. But at the same time there are other scholars who have accepted the hadith, because despite the weakness of Sawwar, it is corroborated by other sources. This is the view of Allama Azizi, Imam Ghazzali and Imam-al-Haramai. However, this controversy relates to the above narration which attributes this statement to the Holy Prophet, Sall-Allahu alayhi wa sallam, but there is no dispute among the scholars of hadith in that the same principle has been enunciated by a number of Sahabah like Sayyidna Fazalah b. Ubaid, Radi-Allahu anhu, whose following statement is reported by Al-Baihaqi:

> كل قرض جر منفعة فهو وجه من وجوه الربا

> "Every loan which derives a benefit is a kind of *riba*."

102. According to Imam Baihaqi, the same principle is also enunciated by Abdullah b. Masud, Ubayy b. Kaab, Abdullah b. Salaam and Abdullah b. Abbas, Radi-Allahu anhum.

103. Nobody has disputed the authenticity of these narrations. Even if it is held that the tradition of Sayyidna Ali, Radi-Allahu anhu, attributing the above statement to the Holy Prophet, Sall-Allahu alayhi wa sallam,, is not authentic, the same principle has been established undoubtedly by several companions of the Holy Prophet, Sall-Allahu alayhi wa sallam. Since the Sahabah were very careful and cautious in mentioning a principle of Shar'iah, and did not normally base any such principle on their personal opinion, it may be presumed that the principle enunciated by them unanimously was, in fact, based on a saying of the Holy Prophet, Sall-Allahu alayhi wa sallam, himself. Even if this presumption is ignored, these reports are sufficient at least to prove that the concept of *riba*, as understood by the Sahabah, includes any increased amount over the principal, however, little it may be. Obviously, the Sahabah were direct addressees of the Holy Qur'an. They were much more aware of the context and the background of the verses of the Holy Qur'an, and therefore, their understanding of a Qur'anic term like *riba* is the most authentic basis for its interpretation.

104. Mr. Riazul Hasan Gilani, the learned counsel for the Federation, raised another objection on the authenticity of the above statement. According to him, this statement suffers from an intrinsic infirmity. If a debtor, he argued, gives an additional

amount at the time of repayment on voluntary basis without any claim from creditor and without a condition in the original contract of loan, it is never held to be *riba* . Yet the words used in the above statement are inclusive of this additional amount also, because the creditor has derived a benefit from his loan, though without his own initiative. It means that the above statement cannot be held as a comprehensive and exclusive definition of *riba* , and such a loose statement should not be attributed to the Holy Prophet, Sall-Allahu alayhi wa sallam, or to his companions.

105. This contention of the learned counsel overlooks the colloquial style of the earlier Arab expressions. Instead of the complex expressions of statutory language, they used to express the sense in simple style, often conveying a detailed concept in shortest possible words. In the above statement they have qualified the word Qarz (loan) with the verb Jerra which lexically means "to pull." The verbal translation of the sentence would be "Every loan which pulls along with it a benefit is *riba* ." Here the underlined words have been added to indicate that *riba* is restricted to a transaction where the loan pulls a benefit along with it in the sense that the contract of loan itself stipulates a benefit for the creditor. The statement has, therefore, excluded any voluntary amount given by the debtor at the time of repayment without pre-determined condition.

106. In the light of the above discussion, there is no force in the contention that the prohibition of *riba* is confined to an excessive rate of interest. The directions of the Holy Qur'an and the Sunnah are quite explicit on the point that any amount, however

little, stipulated in addition to the principal in a transaction of loan is *riba*, hence prohibited.

My Comments 12: The learned Judge's analysis in the foregoing paragraphs (90 to 106) provides further evidence to show that there has got to be a Qur'aanic (divine) definition for *Ar-Riba*. Readers may well see here how, without taking help of the divine sight, we have been groping blindly in the dark - just like the proverbial blind men trying to find out what an elephant was like!

We have seen how the learned Judge has struggled to hammer out a human definition from a myriad of 'Traditions'. As may be seen, these Traditions having been recorded in writing centuries after the events, naturally tend to differ from one another in details and are often contradictory. Some of these are even labelled as weak. Most of these are judgements/opinions given by the Companions in the particular circumstances of the events, the full details of which we do not know.

And the learned Judge in this case is making use of his own judgement to sift the strong from the weak, the reliable from the unreliable, to give us a definition which he considers to be the best.

Can this state of affairs be that of a Religion, Allah Almighty has certified to be perfect!? Please ponder - and ponder deeply!

As regards verse 3.130, my comments under paragraph 22 above may please be perused.

In the course of his analysis here, the learned Judge has also referred to verse 2.179 (see paragraph 93 above). What is translated as 'principal' in this verse is the Arabic term *'ruoosu amwaalikum'*. Here, *'ruoosu'* means 'heads', and one's *'amwaal'* are one's rightfully owned/earned wealth, property and dues. Hence the part of the verse quoted by the learned Judge should more correctly be translated as: "And if you repent, then you are entitled to get back 'heads' of your rightfully owned/earned wealth, property and dues."

And as pointed out in my detailed comments under paragraph 12 above, 'interest' that covers just the Bank's expenses and its reasonable profit margin are the Bank's own *amwaal* falling under the heads of 'expenses' and 'profit'. The Bank would be committing *Ar-Riba,* only if it takes anything over and above its rightful *amwaal.*

Back to Top

Riba al-Fadl and Bank loans

107. Before proceeding further, it will be pertinent to deal with another argument of Mr. Riazul Hasan Gilani, the learned counsel for the Federation, that any increased amount stipulated in a contract of loan right from the beginning does not fall within the definition of *riba al-Qur'an* and that it falls under the definition of *riba al-fadl* . However, if the debtor was not able to pay at the date of maturity for a valid reason, any increased amount imposed

upon the debtor for giving him more time does fall in the definition of *riba al-Qur'an* . Since the most banking transactions of today stipulate interest right from the beginning of the transaction, they are not covered, according to the learned counsel, by the prohibition of *riba al-Qur'an* , they are rather governed by the principles of *riba al-fadl* . He further argued that the enforcement of prohibition of *riba al-fadl* is not the obligation of the State. Its implementation is the responsibility of individual Muslims. It was never enforced in the form of a statute/decree/law by the Holy Prophet, Sall-Allahu alayhi wa sallam, or by the Khulafa-e-Rashedeen and Muslim rulers of the Islamic history. He further claimed that the prohibition of *riba al-fadl* is not applicable to the non-Muslim residents of Islamic State, hence, it is governed by the term "Muslim Personal Law" used in article 203 (b) of the Constitution of Pakistan, and therefore it stands excluded from the jurisdiction of the Federal Shariat Court and the Shariat Appellate Bench of the Supreme Court of Pakistan.

108. This argument of the learned counsel is based on the unprecedented theory that an increase stipulated in the initial transaction of loan is *riba al-fadl* , rather than *riba al-Qur'an* . The first leg of this argument which restricts the definition of *riba al-Qur'an* only to a situation where the creditor increases his claim in exchange of more time given to the debtor after the maturity of the loan has already been fully discussed in para 43 to 54 of this judgment where we have held that *riba al-Qur'an* is not restricted to that situation alone; it rather includes every transaction where an additional amount is claimed over and above the principal,

whether at initial stage or after the maturity. Let us now deal with the second leg of this argument that any increase on the principal stipulated in a contract of loan falls within the definition of *riba al-fadl*. The learned counsel while explaining the concept of *riba al-fadl* went so far that even interest-free loans, he claimed, are covered by the Prohibition of *riba al-fadl*, because according to the hadith prohibiting *riba al-fadl*, the exchange of the six things inter se must be on spot basis. If gold is exchanged for its equal quantity of gold without any addition, but the payment of one side is delayed, it is included in the prohibition of *riba al-fadl*. Therefore, the learned counsel contended, any transaction of loan whereby the repayment of the principal money (which stands for gold or silver) is delayed from one side is *riba al-fadl*, hence, Makruh even though it is returned without any addition, because the transaction of gold for gold (or money for money) is permissible only when two conditions are fulfilled.

(a) That the quantity on both sides are equal

(b) That the exchange is effected on the spot.

109. In an interest-free loan the condition (b) is lacking, while in an interest-based loan both conditions are missing, but both kinds of loan fall within the definition of *riba* al-fadl.

110. This submission of the learned counsel is not tenable at all, because it is based on a major confusion between the transaction of sale and transaction of loan. The learned counsel has equated

the transaction of loan with the transaction of sale. The hadith dealing with *riba* al-fadl refer to a sale transaction, and not to a loan. The exact words of hadith are:

لاتبيعوا الذهب بالذهب إلا مثلا بمثل ...... ولا تبيعوا منها غائبا بناجز

> "Do not sell gold for gold, except in equal quantities...and do not sell the deferred (gold or silver) for the (gold or silver) delivered on the spot."

111. Here the words "Do not sell" are clear to show that the hadith is speaking of a transaction of sale and not of a loan. There are many points of difference between the two transactions. One major difference is that in a sale effected on deferred payment basis, the seller cannot ask the buyer to pay the price before the stipulated date, while in a transaction of a simple interest free loan, the creditor may ask the debtor to repay at any time, and even if a time is stipulated in the transaction of loan, it has only a moral value, and is not binding legally. That is why a transaction of interest-free loan is allowed, while the transaction of gold for gold on deferred payment basis is not permissible. The contention of the learned counsel that even an interest-free loan is covered by *riba* -al-fadl is, therefore, fallacious on the face of it because the Holy Prophet, Sall-Allahu alayhi wa sallam, himself has not only allowed the transactions of interest-free loan but has also practiced them while he never allowed a sale of gold for gold on deferred payment basis. The learned counsel has referred to the Ahadith in which the Holy Prophet, Sall-Allahu

alayhi wa sallam, has condemned borrowing loans without genuine need and refused to pray Janaza of a person who died indebted. But here again, the learned counsel has confused two different issues. The Holy Prophet, Sall-Allahu alayhi wa sallam, did not condemn borrowing loans because the transaction itself was prohibited, but he did so for the simple reason that it is not at all advisable for a person to incur the liability of a loan without a genuine need. Had it been on the basis of the prohibition of the transaction of loan itself, it would have been prohibited for both the lender and the borrower, but obviously advancing a loan has never been held as prohibited. The learned counsel himself referred to a hadith reported by Ibn Majah to the effect that advancing a loan is more meritorious than spending in charity *(Sadaqah)*. It clearly indicates that the transaction of loan in itself is not prohibited as a transaction, however, the people are advised not to incur the liability of a loan without a genuine need. Conversely, a sale of gold for gold or silver for silver on deferred payment basis is a prohibited transaction in itself, and this prohibition is applicable to both the parties, and has never been allowed for any one of them in any case.

112. To sum-up, the Ahadith of *riba al-fadl* are meant to cover the transactions of sale only, and have nothing to do with the transaction of loan which are covered by the rules of *riba al-Qur'an* or *riba al-Jahiliyya* and where it is clearly mentioned that the creditor in a transaction of loan is entitled to claim only his principal amount, and if he does so, it has never been prohibited. It is, therefore, not correct to say that a transaction of interest-bearing loan fixing an amount as interest right from the

beginning of the transaction is covered by the prohibition of *riba al-fadl* rather than the *riba al-Qur'an* and that the banking interest being a transaction of *riba al-fadl* is not haram.

My Comments 13: Please re-read my comments made under paragraph 106, in the context of these paragrphs (107 to 112) also.

Infering a definition for *Ar-Riba* from any individual Tradition is like a blind man (in the proverb quoted in my comments herein above) catching hold of the tail of the elephant and declaring that the elephant is like a rope! We have to have the divine sight of the Qur'aanic definition to get the true and full picture of the *Ar-Riba* elephant.

The background of the Tradition quoted in paragraph 110 above is the conquest of Khyber. Muslims were selling costly gold ornaments, they had got as spoils of war, back to the Jews for a mere 2 or 3 gold dinars. It was in these circumstances that the Prophet (Allah's blessings and peace be upon him) instructed the Muslims not to sell gold for gold, but in equal quantities. This simple economic lesson given by the Prophet, has been taken by our learned scholars to derive a general definition of *Ar-Riba* from!

For further analysis of this and similar other Traditions, you may refer my ebook *ISLAM & INTEREST*.

Back to Top

The Jurisdiction of this Court in the Laws of Interest

113. Having held that the interest charged by the banks on their loans is not *riba al-fadl* (but it is covered by the definition of *riba al-Qur'an*) we need not go into the question whether its prohibition extends to non-Muslims also. However, we would like to note that even if the standpoint of the learned counsel is accepted for a moment, his argument that *riba al-fadl* being applicable to the Muslims only, the laws relating to the banking interest are within the definition of "Muslim Personal Law" as contemplated in article 203(B) of the Constitution of Pakistan and therefore they are outside the jurisdiction of the Federal Shariat Court or the Shariat Appellate Bench of this court, is not sustainable for two obvious reasons:

114. Firstly, the laws under consideration in the present case are the laws as they exists today and not the laws as they should have been in the opinion of the learned counsel. The existing laws do not differentiate between the Muslims and non-Muslims in their application. They are applicable to non-Muslims as well as to the Muslims of the country.

115. Secondly, the notion that laws applicable to Muslims only fall under the definition of "Muslim Personal Law" for the purpose of article 203(B) of the Constitution is, perhaps, based on a previous judgment of this court in the case of Mst. Farishta (PLD 1981 SC 120). But seemingly the learned counsel is not cognizant of the fact that the view taken by the Court in this case was later reviewed in a subsequent judgment of this Court in the case of

Dr. Mahmoodurrahman Faisal Vs. The Government of Pakistan (PLD 1994 SC 607) where it is held that the statute laws, even though applicable only to Muslims in general, do not fall under the term "Muslim Personal Law" for the purpose of article 203 (B) of the Constitution. Therefore, the submission of the learned counsel that the laws relating to bank interest stand excluded from the jurisdiction of this court, is not tenable at any score.

Back to Top

Basic Cause of Prohibition

116. The next argument advanced by some appellants is that the basic cause (illat) of the prohibition of *riba* is Zulm (injustice). The Holy Qur'an says:

وَإِن تُبْتُمْ فَلَكُمْ رُءُوسُ أَمْوَالِكُمْ لَا تَظْلِمُونَ وَلَا تُظْلَمُونَ

> "And if you repent (from charging interest) then you are entitled to your principal. You neither wrong nor be wronged." [Al-Baqarah 2:279]

117. Here the words "neither you wrong nor be wronged" indicate that the basic illat of the prohibition is zulm. It is argued by some appellants that there is no zulm (injustice) at all in charging interest from a rich person who has borrowed money to earn huge profits therewith. Since the basic illat of the prohibition is missing in the commercial interest charged by the banks and the financial institutions, it cannot be held as

prohibited. The same argument was partly advanced by Mr. Khalid M. Ishaque, advocate, who, despite his health constraints, was kind enough to appear in this case as a juris-consult. However, instead of claiming that all the transactions of loan in the present banking system are permissible, Mr. Khalid Ishaq has opined that every individual transaction should be analyzed separately taking into account the surrounding situation of that particular transaction. The focus of the analysis, according to him, should be on the question whether there is an element of zulm in the given situation. In case there is a zulm, the transaction should be taken as *riba* , hence prohibited, but if there is no zulm it should not be taken as haram.

118. We have paid due consideration to this line of argument but were not able to subscribe to it. The argument is based on two assumptions: firstly, that the basic illat of the prohibition is zulm, and secondly, that there is no zulm in the modern interest based transactions or at least there may be some interest-based transactions which have no element of zulm. Both these legs of this argument, after a deeper study, have been found untenable. Let us analyze each one of these two assumptions separately.

Back to Top

The Difference between Illat and Hikmat

119. The first assumption which takes zulm as the basic illat of the prohibition of *riba* is in fact based on confusing the Illat with the Hikmat of a prohibition. It is a well settled principle of Islamic

jurisprudence that there is a big difference between the Illat and the Hikmat of a particular law. The Illat is the basic feature of a transaction without which the relevant law cannot be applied to it, whereas the Hikmat is the wisdom and the philosophy taken into account by the legislator while framing the law or the benefit intended to be drawn by its enforcement. The principle is that the application of a law depends on the Illat and not on the Hikmat. In other words, if the Illat (the basic feature of the transaction) is present in a particular situation while the Hikmat (the wisdom) is not visualized, the law will still be applicable. This principle is recognized in the secular laws also. Let us take a simple example. The law has made it compulsory for the vehicles running on the roads to stop when the red street light is on. The Illat of this law is the red light, while the Hikmat is to avoid the chances of accidents. Now, the law will be applicable whenever the red light is on; its application will not depend on whether or not there is an apprehension of an accident. Therefore, if the red light is on, every vehicle must stop, even though the roads of both sides have no other traffic at all. In this particular case, the basic wisdom (hikmat) of the law is not discernable, because there is no apprehension of any accident in any way. Still the law will be applicable in its full force, because the red light which was the real Illat of the law is present. To cite another example, the Holy Qur'an has prohibited liquor. The Illat of its prohibition is intoxication but the Hikmat of this prohibition has been mentioned by the Holy Qur'an in the following words:

إِنَّمَا يُرِيدُ ٱلشَّيْطَٰنُ أَن يُوقِعَ بَيْنَكُمُ ٱلْعَدَٰوَةَ وَٱلْبَغْضَآءَ فِى ٱلْخَمْرِ وَٱلْمَيْسِرِ وَيَصُدَّكُمْ عَن ذِكْرِ ٱللَّهِ وَعَنِ ٱلصَّلَوٰةِ فَهَلْ أَنتُم مُّنتَهُونَ ۝

"The Satan definitely intends to inculcate enmity and hatred between you by means of liquor and gambling, and wants to prevent you from remembering Allah. So would you not desist?" (5:91)

120. The philosophy of the prohibition of liquor and gambling given by the Holy Qur'an in this verse is that liquor inculcates enmity and hatred between people and it prevents them from remembering Allah. Can one say that he has been using liquor for a long time but it never resulted in having enmity with anyone, and therefore, the basic Illat of the prohibition being not present, he should be allowed to use liquor? Or can one reasonably argue that drinking wine has never prevented him from offering prayers at their due times, and therefore, the basic cause of prohibition mentioned by the Holy Qur'an being absent, the drinking should be held as permissible. Obviously, no one can accept these arguments because the enmity and hatred referred to by the Holy Qur'an in the above verse is not intended to be the Illat of the prohibition. It simply spells out some bad results which the liquor and gambling often produce. They have been mentioned as a Hikmat and the philosophy of the prohibition, but the prohibition itself does not depend on these results. It is in the same way that after prohibiting the transaction of *riba*, the Holy Qur'an has mentioned the Zulm as a Hikmat or a philosophy of the prohibition, but it does not mean

that prohibition will not be applicable if the element of Zulm appears to be missing in a particular case. The Illat (the basic feature) on which the prohibition is based is the excess claimed over and above the principal in a transaction of loan, and as soon as this Illat is present, the prohibition will follow regardless of whether the philosophy of the law is or is not visible in a particular transaction.

121. Another point worth mentioning here is that the Illat of a law is always something determinable by hard and fast definition which leaves no room for a dispute as to whether the Illat is or is not available. Any relative term which is ambiguous in nature cannot be held to be the Illat of a particular law because its existence being susceptible to doubts and disputes, it would defeat the very purpose of the law. The Zulm (Injustice) is a relative and rather ambiguous term the exact definition of which is very difficult to ascertain. Every person may have his own view about what is or what is not Zulm. All the disputing political and economic systems of the world, in fact, claimed to abolish Zulm, but what was regarded as Zulm in one system has been held as justified in another. The communist theory of economy is of the firm view that the private property in itself is a Zulm, while the capitalist theory asserts that abolishing private property is the zulm. Such an ambiguous term is not competent to be the Illat of a particular law.

122. Mr. Khalid M. Ishaque, advocate, who appeared as a juris-consult in this case, adopted another approach. According to him, non-availability of a hard and fast definition of 'zulm' or

riba should be taken as a blessing from Allah, for it provides elasticity to the Muslims of every age to determine what is zulm in the given situations of their time. In his written statement the learned jurisconsult has expressed himself in the following words:

>a) Misdirected efforts towards definition-making ought to be discontinued. Absence of definition of *riba* in the Qur'an should be accepted as such and rather be looked upon as a mercy for mankind. The deliberate omission of a rigid definition would propel Muslims to come up with their own guiding and evolving principles of identifying zulm in space-time situations. Economic conditions are not static and nor are human situations.
>
>b) A sound economic policy ought to include "all purposeful governmental action whose actual and professed primary objective is the improvement of the economic welfare of the whole population for which government is responsible, not of some segment of that population." The Islamic concept of economy is not inimical or dissimilar to the above. As such, an Islamic approach should neither be insulated and detached from an economistic approach/program nor should it be in

ignorance of the same as they need not be mutually exclusive.

Jurists should not close their mind to the possibility that both can be synergized to arrive at the most beneficial and fair outcome. Very typically, whenever Muslim jurists have not kept themselves abreast with or informed of contemporary disciplines (economics is a case in point), they have a tendency to become averse to it, treat it with suspicion, regard it as a hazard and simply label it as un-Islamic to avoid study of the same.

123. We paid due consideration to this approach, but with due respect to the learned juris-consult, this argument seems to overlook some fundamental points:

124. Firstly, the learned juris-consult has taken the deliberate omission of a rigid definition of *riba* (by the Holy Qur'an) as a mercy for mankind. This argument appears to presume that the Holy Qur'an normally gives definitions of the acts prohibited by it, but in the case of *riba* the Holy Qur'an deliberately omitted to give a rigid definition. The fact, however, is that the Holy Qur'an has hardly given a legal definition to any one of its prohibitions. No definition is given for *khamr* (liquor), nor for *qimar* (gambling) nor for *zina* (adultery or fornication) nor for theft, nor for robbery, nor for *kufr*. Similarly the Holy Qur'an did not define its imperatives like Salat, Sawm

(fasting), Zakah, Hajj or Jihad. Should we, then, say that none of these concepts has a specific meaning and all these injunctions are therefore subject to ever-changing whims based on "space-time situations"? The Holy Qur'an, in fact, did not give legal definitions to these concepts because their meanings were too obvious to need an express definition. Some ancillary details of these concepts might have not been so clear and might have given rise to differences of opinion, but it does not mean that the basic concept of all these injunctions has been floated in void or vacuum, having no specific sense at all.

125. Secondly, the learned juris-consult has succinctly outlined the basic features of a sound economic policy in the italicized portion of the above extract. One can hardly question its soundness. Almost all the economic systems claim to strive for the same objectives, but the question is how to achieve them? It is the answer to this very question that has divided different economic systems into conflicting rivals. The learned juris-consult suggests that "Islamic approach should not be insulated and detached from an economistic approach/program." The suggestion seems to be substantially reasonable, but when this suggestion is given in the context of leaving the definition of *riba* unsettled and "evolving principles of identifying zulm in space-time situations" it apparently means that it is the pure economic approach which will play a decisive role in identifying zulm in a particular situation and in turn determining what is halal or haram in Shar'iah. Once it is taken for granted, the question is "which economic approach"? There are numerous theories,

conflicting with each other, but each one of them pretending to race towards the sound economic policy of "improving the economic welfare of the whole population." The basic economic goals of a welfare economy are recognized by almost everyone thinking on economic subjects. However, it is the strategy for translating these objectives into reality that makes a big difference. The Islamic strategy to achieve these goals is neither too narrow to accommodate the ever-changing needs of the humanity or too biased to interact with the modern thought, nor is it too dependent on the modern theories to make its own way towards these goals. Islam has no problem in welcoming any constructive suggestion from whatever quarter it may have come, but at the same time it has its own principles on which no compromise is possible, because they are based on divine guidance, the most distinct feature of the Islamic economy that draws the line of difference between the Islamic and secular economies - and the prohibition of *riba* is one of those basic principles. To leave this principle at the mercy of the secular economic policies is, therefore, like placing the cart before the horse.

126. Thirdly, abolishing zulm (injustice) is not the hikmat or purpose of the prohibition of *riba* alone. It is the reson' detre of most of the Islamic injunctions relating to business and trade. But whenever the Holy Qur'an and Sunnah gave a specific command or prohibition in these areas, they did not rely on the rational assessment of the people, nor did they leave these transactions at the mercy of human reason to decide whether or not they have an element of Zulm. If the Holy Qur'an and the Sunnah intended to entrust such a decision

to the human intellect alone, they would have not revealed such a long list of commands and prohibitions; they would have rather issued one single command that all people must avoid zulm in all their transactions. But the Holy Qur'an and Sunnah were cognizant of the fact that human reason, despite its wide capabilities, cannot claim to have unlimited power to reach the truth. After all, it has some limits beyond which it either cannot properly work or may fall prey to errors. There are many areas of human life where "reason" is often confused with "desires" and where unhealthy instincts, under the garb of rational arguments, misguide the humanity and demonstrate the unjust attitudes in the disguised form of justice. It is these areas where human reason needs the guidance of divine revelation, and it is the divine revelation which finally decides as to which human attitude actually falls within the limits of "zulm" or injustice, even though it appears to be just in the eyes of some secular rationalists, and it is in such issues that the divine revelations come with a specific command that prevails upon the rational arguments advanced by differing opinions. That is exactly what happened in the case of *riba* . The secular rationalists were fully content with their belief that *riba* transactions practiced by them were quite justified, because the income they earn through interest is very similar to the profit they earn through sales. That is why they confronted the prohibition of *riba* by their rational argument quoted by the Holy Qur'an in the following words:

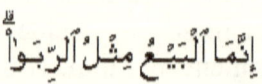

> Sale is nothing but similar to *riba* .
> [Al-Baqarah 2:275]

127. They intended that if a profit claimed in a transaction of sale is just and lawful, there is no reason why an interest claimed in a transaction of loan is held to be unjust and unlawful. In answer to this argument of theirs, the Holy Qur'an could have mentioned the difference between interest and profit in pure logical manner, and could have explained how the profit in a sale is justified while the interest is not. The Holy Qur'an could have also spelled out the evil consequences of *riba* on the economy. But this line of argument was intentionally avoided, and the brief and simple answer given by the Holy Qur'an was:

$$وَأَحَلَّ ٱللَّهُ ٱلْبَيْعَ وَحَرَّمَ ٱلرِّبَوٰاْ$$

> "Allah has allowed the sale and has prohibited interest." [Al-Baqarah 2:275]

128. The hint given in this verse is that the question whether these transactions have an element of injustice is not left to be decided by human reason alone, because the reason of different individuals may come up with different answers and no absolute conclusion of universal application may be arrived at on the basis of pure rational arguments. The correct principle, therefore, is that once a particular transaction is held by Allah to be haram, there is no room for disputing it on the basis of pure rational argumentation because Allah's knowledge

and wisdom encompasses all those points which are not accessible to ordinary reason. If the human reason was fully competent to reach the correct decision unanimously in each and every issue, no divine revelation would be called for. There is a wide area of human conduct in which the Creator did not give a specific command. It is this area where human reason can well play its role, but it should not be burdened to play the role of a rival to the express divine injunctions.

129. The Qur'anic verse referring to zulm (Injustice) in the context of *riba* should be studied in this perspective. The exact words of the verse are:

وَإِن تُبْتُمْ فَلَكُمْ رُءُوسُ أَمْوَالِكُمْ لَا تَظْلِمُونَ وَلَا تُظْلَمُونَ

"And if you repent (from claiming *riba*), then you are entitled to get your principal back. Neither you wrong nor be wronged." [Al-Baqarah 2:279]

130. Before referring to zulm, the Qur'anic verse has laid down the precise principle that no one can be deemed to have repented from the practice of *riba* unless he has withdrawn from claiming any additional amount over and above the principal, but on the other hand he is fully entitled to get back his principal, and his debtor is bound to pay him the full amount of loan. If the debtor will not pay the principal, he will be committing injustice against the creditor, and if the creditor will claim something more than the principal, he will be committing injustice to the debtor.

131. Thus the Holy Qur'an did not leave it to the assessment of the parties to decide what is injustice and what is not. Instead, the Holy Book itself has precisely decided what is injustice for each one of the two parties in a transaction of loan. Therefore, the notion that the permissibility of different transactions of interest should be judged on the basis of human assessment is tantamount to defeating the very purpose of the revelation and is not, therefore, acceptable.

My Comments 14: Adopting the terminology of the learned Judge, we may concede that eradication of injustice is the Hikmat - and not the Illat - of the divine injunction on *Ar-Riba*. But then, what is the Illat?

The learned Judge had already earlier ruled that the the meaning of the Qur'aanic term 'Ar-Riba' is Interest, i.e. any additional amount charged on the debtor, over and above the loan taken by him. In this meaning lies the Illat of the divine Law on *Ar-Riba*. Let us now examine whether this Illat does have the distinctive characteristics therefor, that are specified by the Judge himself.

No doubt, the Red Light is the Illat of the Traffic Law. The makers of this Law specifically and unambiguously laid down in the relevant statute that on seeing the red light, all vehicular traffic should stop. This is specifically made known to each and every driver, before he receives the driving licence. This colour is purposely chosen because it is very distinctive and there cannot be any ambiguity about it in any driver's mind.

Now take the case of Interest, which the learned Judge says is the meaning of *Ar-Riba*, and therefore the Illat of the divine Law on *Ar-Riba*. Has Allah Ta'ala, the Maker of this divine Law, so specifically and unambiguously laid down in the relevant statute, i.e. the Qur'aan, that Interest is the Illat of this divine Law? The obvious answer to this question is an emphatic <u>NO</u>.

To quote the learned Judge himself, "Another point worth mentioning here is that the Illat of a law is always something determinable by hard and fast definition which leaves no room for a dispute as to whether the Illat is or is not available." By this standard, the Red Light is the indisputable Illat of the Traffic Law. To the best of my knowledge and belief, there has never ever been a dispute on what Red Light means.

But we cannot say the same thing about the meaning of *Ar-Riba* as Interest. The very Court case, in which the learned Judge has given this judgement, is proof enough that it is not the ' hard and fast definition which leaves no room for a dispute ' and therefore does not qualify to be the Illat of the divine Law on *Ar-Riba!*

Readers may also go through my detailed comments under paragraph 12 above, in this context. And as regards interpretation of verse 2.279, my comments thereon under paragraph 106 above may please be seen.

Therefore the indisputable Illat of the divine Law on *Ar-Riba* has to be the definition (viz., the increase effected in one's own *amwaal* by usurping the *amwaal* of other people in any transaction) of the Arabic term given in verse 30.39. There is no question of this definition being subject to any dispute because it is divinely given and ' there is no room for disputing it on the basis of pure rational argumentation because Allah's knowledge and wisdom encompasses all those points which are not accessible to ordinary reason' as the Judge himself learnedly observes in paragraph 128 above.

In verse 2.275, a quote of those indulging in *Ar-Riba* is given. This quote has been translated as "Sale is nothing but similar to *riba* " and referred to by the learned Judge in paragraph 126 above. The learned Judge is obviously at pains to show that his interpretation of *Ar-Riba* as Interest is correct and that the quote was of those who protested against Interest being prohibited. Had it been so, the Interest-takers would have naturally stated the converse: *"Riba* is nothing but similar to sale." The Judge is aware of this lacuna in his arguments. And to cover up the injustice involved in prohibiting Interest, as such, he has resorted to the plea that ' the question whether these transactions have an element of injustice is not left to be decided by human reason alone .'

The fact of the matter is that the Judge, with all my respects to him, had to resort to the laboured argument because of the weakness of his ruling that 'Ar-Riba' is Interest. The quote in verse 2.275, is obviously of those who likened any Allah-permitted sale/trade/business ('bai'a' in

Arabic) to 'Ar-Riba', like those who, in modern days, say, "Banking business is 'Ar-Riba'."

In paragraph 124, the learned Judge says that the Qur'aan has also not given any definition for 'Az-Zakaat'. This is blatantly untrue, because it is very much defined in the very same verse 30.39. It has been defined as that which is given away just for the pleasure of Allah. It is because of this clear definition that no charity given by an atheist can qualify to be called as 'Az-Zakaat'.

With reference to the Judge's analysis of the question of jurisdiction, it may be mentioned here that the injunction against 'Ar-Riba' is primarily applicable to Muslims. This is so because verse 2.278 is specifically addressed to the Believers. In certain cases of 'Ar-Riba', the injunction cannot be honestly implemented by non-believers. It is essentially a matter between an individual and his/her Creator, like that of fasting during the month of Ramadhaan. However, certain other aspects of the Law, as for example, prohibition of corruption among Government employees, can be enforced by the State by enacting special legislation in that regard.

Back to Top

Rationale of the Prohibition of *Riba*

132. Now we come to the second leg of the argument which contends that no element of injustice is found in the commercial or banking interest.

133. Although, in the light of the above discussion, the Holy Qur'an has itself decided what injustice in a transaction of loan is, and it is not necessary that everybody finds out all the elements of injustice in a *riba* transaction, yet the evil consequences of interest were never so evident in the past than they are today. Injustice in a personal consumption loan was restricted to a debtor only, while the injustice brought by the modern interest affects the economy as a whole. A detailed account of the rationale of the prohibition of *riba* would, in fact, require a separate volume, but for the purpose of brevity we would concentrate on three aspects of the issue:

(a) The logic of the prohibition on theoretical ground

(b) The evil effects of interest on production

(c) The evil effects of interest on distribution.

134. On pure theoretical ground, we would like to focus on two basic issues; firstly on the nature of money and secondly on the nature of a loan transaction.

Back to Top

Nature of Money

135. One of the wrong presumptions on which all theories of interest are based is that money has been treated as a commodity. It is, therefore, argued that just as a merchant can sell his commodity for a

higher price than his cost, he can also sell his money for a higher price than its face value, or just as he can lease his property and can charge a rent against it, he can also lend his money and can claim interest thereupon.

136 . Islamic principles, however, do not subscribe to this presumption. Money and commodity have different characteristics and therefore they are treated differently. The basic points of difference between money and commodity are as follows:

(a) Money has no intrinsic utility. It cannot be utilized in direct fulfillment of human needs. It can only be used for acquiring some goods or services. A commodity, on the other hand, has intrinsic utility and can be utilized directly without exchanging it for some other thing.

(b) The commodities can be of different qualities while money has no quality except that it is a measure of value or a medium of exchange. Therefore, all the units of money of the same denomination, are hundred per cent equal to each other. An old and dirty note of Rs.1000/= has the same value as a brand new note of Rs.1000/=.

(c) In commodities, the transactions of sale and purchase are effected on an identified particular commodity. If A has purchased a particular car by pin-pointing it, and seller has agreed, he deserves to receive the same car. The seller cannot compel him to take the delivery of another car, though of the same type or quality.

Money, on the contrary, cannot be pin-pointed in a transaction of exchange. If A has purchased a commodity from B by showing him a particular note of Rs.1000/- he can still pay him another note of the same denomination.

137. Based on these basic differences, Islamic Shar'iah has treated money differently from commodities, especially on two scores:

138. Firstly, money (of the same denomination) is not held to be the subject-matter of trade, like other commodities. Its use has been restricted to its basic purpose i.e. to act as a medium of exchange and a measure of value.

139. Secondly, if for exceptional reasons, money has to be exchanged for money or it is borrowed, the payment on both sides must be equal, so that it is not used for the purpose it is not meant for i.e. trade in money itself.

140. Imam Al-Ghazzali (d.505 A.H.) the renowned jurist and philosopher of the Islamic history has discussed the nature of money in an early period when the Western theories of money were non-existent. He says:

"The creation of dirhams and dinars (money) is one of the blessings of Allah.... They are stones having no intrinsic usufruct or utility, but all human beings need them, because every body needs a large number of commodities for his eating, wearing etc, and often he does not have what he needs and does have what he needs not.. Therefore, the transactions of exchange are inevitable. But there must be a measure on the basis of which price can be determined, because the exchanged commodities are neither of the same type, nor of the same measure which can determine how much quantity of one commodity is a just price for another. Therefore, all these commodities need a mediator to judge their exact value.... Allah Almighty has, therefore, created dirhams and dinars (money) as judges and mediators between all commodities so that all objects of wealth are measured through them... and their being the measure of the value of all commodities is based on the fact that they are not an objective in themselves. Had they been an objective in themselves, one could have a specific purpose for keeping them which might have given them more importance according to his intention while the one who had no such purpose would have not given

them such importance and thus the whole system would have been disturbed. That is why Allah has created them, so that they may be circulated between hands and act as a fair judge between different commodities and work as a medium to acquire other things.... So, the one who owns them is as he owns every thing, unlike the one who owns a cloth, because he owns only a cloth, therefore, if he needs food, the owner of the food may not be interested in exchanging his food for cloth, because he may need an animal for example. Therefore, there was needed a thing which in its appearance is nothing, but in its essence is everything. The thing which has no particular form may have different forms in relation to other things like a mirror which has no color, but it reflects every color. The same is the case of money. It is not an objective in itself, but it is an instrument to lead to all objectives...

So, the one who is using money in a manner contrary to its basic purpose is, in fact, disregarding the blessings of Allah. Consequently, whoever hoards money is doing injustice to it and is defeating their actual purpose. He is like the one who detains a ruler in a prison...

> *And whoever effects the transactions of interest on money is, in fact, discarding the blessing of Allah and is committing injustice, because money is created for some other things, not for itself. So, the one who has started trading in money itself has made it an objective contrary to the original wisdom behind its creation, because it is injustice to use money for a purpose other than what it was created for.... If it is allowed for him to trade in money itself, money will become his ultimate goal and will remain detained with him like hoarded money. And imprisoning a ruler or restricting a postman from conveying messages is nothing but injustice."*

141. This brief, yet comprehensive, analysis of the nature of money, undertaken by Imam Al-Ghazzali about nine hundred years ago, is admitted to be true by the economists who came centuries after him. That money is only a medium of exchange and a measure of value is universally accepted by almost all the economists of the world, but unfortunately a large number of these economists failed to recognize the logical outcome of this concept, so clearly elaborated by Imam al-Ghazzali: that money should not be treated as a commodity meant for being traded in. After holding that money is a commodity, the modern economists have plunged into a dilemma that was never resolved satisfactorily. The commodities are classified into the commodities of first order which are normally

termed as "consumption goods" and the commodities of the higher order which are called "productive goods." Since money, having no intrinsic utility, could not be included in "consumption goods" most of the economists had no option but to put it under the category of "production goods", but it was hardly proved by sound logical arguments that money is a "production good." Ludwig Von Mises, the well-known economist of the present century has dealt with the subject in detail. He says:

> *"Of course, if we regard the twofold division of economic goods as exhaustive, we shall have to rest content with putting money in one group or the other. This has been the position of most economists; and since it has seemed altogether impossible to call money a consumption good, there has been no alternative but to call it a production good."*

142. After citing different arguments in support of this view, he comments as follows:

> *"It is true that the majority of economists reckon money among production goods. Nevertheless, arguments from authority are invalid; the proof of a theory is in its reasoning, not in its sponsorship; and with all due respect for the masters, it must be said that they*

> *have not justified their position very thoroughly in the matter."*

143. He then concludes:

> *"Regarded from this point of view, those goods that are employed as money are indeed what Adam Smith called them, 'dead stock, which... produces nothing.'"*

144. The author has then expressed his inclination to the Kien's theory that money is neither a consumption good nor a production good; it is a medium of exchange.

145. The logical result of this finding would have been that money should not be taken as an instrument that gives birth to more money on daily basis, nor should it have been taken as a tradable commodity, when it is exchanged for another money of the same denomination, because once it is accepted that money is neither consumption good nor production good, and that it is merely a medium of exchange, then there remains no room for making itself an object of profitable trade, for it will be like a mediator himself has been made a party. But, perhaps due to the overwhelming domination of interest-based monetary system, many economists did not proceed any further in this direction.

146. Imam Al-Ghazzali, on the other hand, has taken the concept of "medium of exchange" to its logical end. He has concluded that when money is exchanged for money of the same denomination, it

should never be made an instrument generating profit by such exchange.

147. This approach of Imam al-Ghazzali, fully backed by the clear directives of the Holy Qur'an and Sunnah, has however been admitted to be true by some realistic scholars, even in societies dominated by interest. Many of them after facing the severe consequences of their financial system based on trade in money have admitted that their economic plight was caused, inter alia, by the fact that money was not restricted to be used for its primary function as a medium of exchange.

148. During the horrible depression of 1930s, an "Economic Crisis Committee" was formed by Southampton Chamber of Commerce in January 1933. The Committee consisted of ten members headed by Mr. E. Dennis Mundy. In its report the committee had discussed the root causes of the calamitous depression in national and international trade and had suggested different measures to overcome the problem. After discussing the pitfalls of the existing financial system, one of the committee's recommendation was that:

> "In order to ensure that money performs its true function of operating as a means of exchange and distribution, it is desirable that it should cease to be traded as a commodity."

149. This real nature of money which should have been appreciated as a fundamental principle of the financial system remained neglected for centuries,

but it is now increasingly recognized by the modern economists. Prof. John Gray (of Oxford University), in his recent work False Dawn has remarked as follows:

> "Most significantly, perhaps transactions on foreign exchange markets have now reached the astonishing sum of around $1.2 trillion a day, over fifty times the level of the world trade. Around 95 percent of these transactions are speculative in nature, many using complex new derivative's financial instruments based on futures and options. According to Michael Albert, the daily volume of transactions on the foreign exchange markets of the world holds some $900 billions - equal to France's annual GDP and some $200 million more than the total foreign currency reserves of the world central banks.
>
> This virtual financial economy has a terrible potential for disrupting the underlying real economy as seen in the collapse in 1995 of Earings, Britain's oldest bank."

The size of derivatives mentioned by John Gray was, by the way, of their daily transactions. The size of their total worth, however, is much greater. It is mentioned by Richard Thomson in his "Apocalypse Roulette" in the following words:

> "Financial derivatives have grown, more or less from standing starting in the early 1970s, to a $64 trillion (that's $64,000,000,000,000) industry by 1996. How do you imagine a number that big? You could say that if you laid all those dollar bills end to end, they would stretch from here to the sun sixty-six times, or to the moon 25,900 times;"

150. James Robertson observes in his latest work, Transforming Economic Life in the following words:

> "Today's money and finance system is unfair, ecologically destructive and economically inefficient. The money-must-grow imperative drives production (and thus consumption) to higher than necessary levels. It skews economic effort towards money out of money, and against providing real services and goods...
>
> ...(It) also results in a massive world-wide diversion of effort away from providing useful goods and services, into making money out of money. At least 95% of the billions of dollars transferred daily around the world are for purely financial transactions, unlinked to transactions in the real economy."

151. This is exactly what Imam Al-Ghazzali had pointed out nine hundred years ago. The evil results of such an unnatural trade have been further explained by him at another place, in the following words:

> *"Riba (interest) is prohibited because it prevents people from undertaking real economic activities. This is because when a person having money is allowed to earn more money on the basis of interest, either in spot or in deferred transactions, it becomes easy for him to earn without bothering himself to take pains in real economic activities. This leads to hampering the real interests of the humanity, because the interests of the humanity cannot be safeguarded without real trade skills, industry and construction."*

152. It seems that Imam Al-Ghazzali had, in that early age, pointed out the phenomenon of monetary factors prevailing on production, creating a wide gap between the supply of money and the supply of real goods which has emerged in the later days as the major cause of inflation, almost the same "terrible potential" of trading in money as explained by John Gray and James Robertson in their above extracts. We will examine this aspect a little later, but what is important at this point is the fact that money, being a medium of exchange and a measure of value cannot be taken as a "production good" which yields profit on daily basis, as is presumed by

the theories of interest. This is a mediator and it should be left to play this exclusive role. To make it an object of profitable trade disturbs the whole monetary system and brings a plethora of economic and moral hazards to the whole society.

My Comments 15: It is obviously a case of mistaken identities. *Ar-Riba,* as defined in the Qur'aan, is the real villain of the piece. Interest, poor thing, is blamed, instead, for all the economic ills!

Money, howsoever may the economists classify it, is no doubt an item of immense utility. We utilise it to purchase things. The money that we own, thus represents the current purchasing power with us. It represents, in other words, the current value of the demat (dematerialised) wealth, other than the material wealth like landed properties, ornaments etc., with us. It is, in a way, like the demat accounts we nowadays have for Company shares we own.

In our earthly lives, situations may sometimes arise wherein there is a genuine need to borrow money. The Qur'aan recognises this need and has laid down certain parameters in which to do it. As there is a genuine need to borrow, there is a genuine need of someone who can lend. Lending is therefore a necessary social activity. It is an activity, in other words, for supply of a lawful necessity, viz., the purchasing power. All activities for supply of such necessities are businesses *(Al-Bai'a)* specifically allowed in the Qur'aan [Q: 2.275].

The Qur'aan, therefore, condemns, in the same verse, those who say that such an Allah-permitted business is like *Ar-Riba*

If the Interest charged by a bonafide bank is restricted to its expenses plus reasonable profit, then these are its own *amwaal* and do not come under the mischief of *Ar-Riba*. Such Interest has to be construed as banafide service charges for the service the bank renders in making the purchasing power available to the borrower. It should not be construed as trading in money and profiteering thereby. It is not such bonafide Interest that causes the economic ills, the learned Judge and the economists speak about.

But if the bank invests the funds at its disposal in speculations at the stockmarket and makes a quick buck because of the manipulations of the slick operators there, then that would amount to trading in money! It is this quick buck that really is *Ar-Riba*. The quick buck is not the bank's rightful *amwaal*. It has usurped it from that of the buyers of the shares, prices of which were skewed up by manipulation.

Sadly, the learned Judge has grossly mistaken the identity of the real culprit!

And I know of Muslims, known to be very religious, who would shun the bank Interest as *haraam*, but would gladly accept the quick buck saying that it is obtained by *halaal* trading of shares! No wonder, the Qur'aan describes such persons as being under the spell of the Satan!

Back to Top

The Nature of Loan

153. Another major difference between the secular capitalist system and the Islamic principles is that under the former system, loans are purely commercial transactions meant to yield a fixed income to the lenders. Islam, on the other hand, does not recognize loans as income-generating transactions. They are meant only for those lenders who do not intend to earn a worldly return through them. They, instead, lend their money either on humanitarian grounds to achieve a reward in the Hereafter, or merely to save their money through a safer hand. So far as investment is concerned, there are several other modes of investment like partnership etc which may be used for that purpose. The transactions of loan are not meant for earning income.

154. The basic philosophy underlying this scheme is that the one who is offering his money to another person has to decide whether:

>(a) He is lending money to him as a sympathetic act or

>(b) He is lending money to the borrower, so that his principal may be saved or

(c) He is advancing his money to share the profits of the borrower.

155. In the former two cases (a) and (b) he is not entitled to claim any additional amount over and above the principal, because in case (a) he has offered financial assistance to the borrower on humanitarian grounds or any other sympathetic considerations, and in case (b) his sole purpose is to save his money and not to earn any extra income.

156. However, if his intention is to share the profits of the borrower, as in case (c), he shall have to share his loss also, if he suffers a loss. In this case, his objective cannot be served by a transaction of loan. He will have to undertake a joint venture with the opposite party, whereby both of them will have a joint stake in the business and will share its outcome on fair basis. Conversely, if the intent of sharing the profit of the borrower is designed on the basis of an interest-based loan, it will mean that the financier wants to ensure his own profit, while he leaves the profit of the borrower at the mercy of the actual outcome of the business. There may be a situation where the business of the borrower totally fails. In this situation he will not only bear the whole loss of the business, but he also will have to pay interest to the lender, meaning thereby that the profit or interest of the financier is guaranteed at the price of the destructive loss of the borrower, which is obviously a glaring injustice.

157. On the other hand, if the business of the borrower earns huge profits, the financier should have shared in the profit in reasonable proportion, but in an interest-based system, the profit of the

financier is restricted to a fixed rate of return which is governed by the forces of supply and demand of money and not on the actual profits produced on the ground. This rate of interest may be much less than the reasonable proportion a financier might have deserved, had it been a joint venture. In this case the major part of the profit is secured by the borrower, while the financier gets much less than deserved by his input in the business, which is another form of injustice.

158. Thus, financing a business on the basis of interest creates an unbalanced atmosphere which has the potential of bringing injustice to either of the two parties in different situations. That is the wisdom for which the Shar'iah did not approve an interest based loan as a form of financing.

159. Once the interest is banned, the role of "loans" in commercial activities becomes very limited, and the whole financing structure turns out to be equity-based and backed by real assets. In order to limit the use of loans, the Shar'iah has permitted to borrow money only in cases of dire need, and has discouraged the practice of incurring debts for living beyond one's means or to grow one's wealth. The well-known event that the Holy Prophet, Sall-Allahu alayhi wa sallam, refused to offer the funeral prayer (salat-ul janazah) of a person who died indebted was, in fact, to establish the principle that incurring debt should not be taken as a natural or ordinary phenomenon of life. It should be the last thing to be resorted to in the course of economic activities. This is one of the reasons for which interest has been prohibited, because, given the prohibition of interest, no one will be agreeable to

advance a loan without a return for unnecessary expenses of the borrower or for his profitable projects. It will leave no room for unnecessary expenses incurred through loans. The profitable ventures, on the other hand, will be designed on the basis of equitable participation and thus the scope of loans will remain restricted to a narrow circle.

160. Conversely, once the interest is allowed, and advancing loans, in itself, becomes a form of profitable trade, the whole economy turns into a debt-oriented economy which not only dominates over the real economic activities and disturbs its natural functions by creating frequent shocks, but also puts the whole mankind under the slavery of debt. It is no secret that all the nations of the world, including the developed countries, are drowned in national and foreign debts to the extent that the amount of payable debts in a large number of countries exceeds their total income. Just to take one example of UK, the household debt in 1963 was less than 30% of total annual income. In 1997, however, the percentage of household debt rose up to more than 100% of the total income. It means that the household debt throughout the country, embracing rich and poor alike, represents more than the entire gross annual incomes of the country. Consumers have borrowed, and made purchases against their future earnings, equivalent to more than the entirety of their annual incomes. Peter Warburton, one of the UK's most respected financial commentators and a past winner of economic forecasting awards, has commented on this situation as follows:

"The credit and capital markets have grown too rapidly, with too little transparency and accountability. Prepare for an explosion that will rock the western financial system to its foundation."

<u>My Comments 16</u>: It is important that we properly understand the basics of economically sound and valid income generation.

When a trader sells his goods, it's not basically the goods that get him his earnings. It's really the efforts he has put in to make the goods conveniently available to his customers that generate and justify his earnings. If his earnings exceed justfiable limits, he would be eating into the *amwaal* of his customers and thus committing Ar-Riba. That is why the Qur'aan says, "Allah has permitted *Al-Bai'a* (business), and prohibited *Ar-Riba...*" [Q: 2.275]

Similarly, when a bank gives a loan, it's not the loan as such that gets the bank its earnings. It's really the huge corporate effort, in collecting the funds, keeping the proper accounts, checking the antecedents of the applicants for loan and granting loans after proper scrutiny, that generates and justifies the bank's earnings, which is contained in the Interest it charges. It would be unjust to deny the bank its due and justifiable earnings on this account. It would be un-Islamic to do so, in the light of verse 2.275.

And just as the trader has to sell his goods at fixed prices, the bank too has to take interest at fixed rates, commensurate with the expenses incurred and its justifiable earnings. That Islam does not permit charging of such interest at fixed rates, is a myth.

It is not the banks' charging interests at reasonable and justifiable rates, that creates the economic imbalances in society. It is the *Ar-Riba* that the banks commit by charging interests at more than the justifiable limits, or by investing their funds in dubious activities like speculation that the imbalances are created. And this is how "The credit and capital markets have grown too rapidly, with too little transparency and accountability" as Peter Warburton has stated.

One can always give loans at zero rate of interest, or one may even write the loans off in deserving cases, on humanitarian grounds. Allah Ta'ala promises rich rewards for those who do so, to seek His pleasure. But such acts of charity should not be confused with 'Ar-Riba'. Good banks do make provisions for writing off of loans in deserving cases, but if they cannot afford to be charitable in all cases, they cannot be accused of committing 'Ar-Riba' on that ground.

Back to Top

Overall Effects of Interest

161. Interest-based loans have a persistent tendency in favor of the rich and against the interests of the common people. It carries adverse effects on production and allocation of resources as well as on

distribution of wealth. Some of these effects are the following:

Back to Top

(a) Evil Effects on Allocation of Resources

162. Loans in the present banking system are advanced mainly to those who, on the strength of their wealth, can offer satisfactory collateral. Dr. M, Umar Chapra (Senior Economic Advisor to Saudi Arabian Monetary Agency) who appeared in this case as a juris-consult has summarized the effects of this practice in the following words:

> "Credit, therefore, tends to go to those who, according to Lester Thurow, are 'lucky rather than smart or meritocratic. The banking system thus tends to reinforce the unequal distribution of capital. Even Morgen Guarantee Trust Company, sixth largest bank in the U.S. has admitted that the banking system has failed to 'finance either maturing smaller companies or venture capitalist' and 'though awash with funds, is not encouraged to deliver competitively priced funding to any but the largest, most cash-rich companies. Hence, while deposits come from a broader cross-section of the population, their benefit goes mainly to the rich."

(Dr. Chapra's written statement under the caption "Why has Islam prohibited Interest?" P.18)

163. The veracity of this statement can be confirmed by the fact that according to the statistics issued by the State Bank of Pakistan in September 1999, 9269 account holders out of 2,184,417 (only 0.4243% of total account holders) have utilized Rs.438.67 billion which is 64.5% of total advances as of end December 1998.

Back to Top

(b) Evil Effects on Production

164. Since in an interest-based system funds are provided on the basis of strong collateral and the end-use of the funds does not constitute the main criterion for financing, it encourages people to live beyond their means. The rich people do not borrow for productive projects only, but also for conspicuous consumption. Similarly, governments borrow money not only for genuine development programs, but also for their lavish expenditure and for projects motivated by their political ambitions rather than being based on sound economic assessment. Non-project-related borrowings, which were possible only in an interest-based system have thus helped in nothing but increasing the size of our debts to a horrible extent. According to the budget of 1998/99 in our country 46 percent of the total government spending is devoted to debt-servicing, while only 18% is allocated for development which includes education, health and infrastructure.

Back to Top

(c) Evil Effects on Distribution

165. We have already pointed out that when business is financed on the basis of interest, it may bring injustice either to the borrower if he suffers a loss, or to the financier if the debtor earns huge profits. Although both situations are equally possible in an interest-based system, and there are many examples where the payment of interest has brought total ruin to the small traders, yet in our present banking system, the injustice brought to the financier is more pronounced and much more disturbing to the equitable distribution of wealth.

166. In the context of modern capitalist system, it is the banks which advance depositors' money to the industrialists and traders. Almost all the giant business ventures are mostly financed by the banks and financial institutions. In numerous cases the funds deployed by the big entrepreneurs from their own pocket are much less than the funds borrowed by them from the common people through banks and financial institutions. If the entrepreneurs having only ten million of their own, acquire 90 million from the banks and embark on a huge profitable enterprise, it means that 90% of the projects is created by the money of the depositors while only 10% was generated by their own capital. If these huge projects bring enormous profits, only a small proportion (of interest which normally ranges between 2% to 10% in different countries) will go to the depositors whose input in the projects was 90% while all the rest will be secured by the big entrepreneurs whose real contribution to the

projects was not more than 10%. Even this small proportion given to the depositors is taken back by these big entrepreneurs, because all the interest paid by them is included in the cost of their production and comes back to them through the increased prices. The net result in this case is that all the profits of the big enterprises is earned by the persons whose own financial input does not exceed 10% of the total investment, while the people whose financial contribution was as high as 90% get nothing in real terms, because the amount of interest given to them is often repaid by them through the increased prices of the products, and therefore, in a number of cases the return received by them becomes negative in real terms.

167. While this phenomenon is coupled with the fact, already mentioned, that 64.5% of total advances went only to 0.4243% of total account holders, it means that the profits generated mostly by the money of millions of people went almost exclusively to 9,269 borrowers. One can imagine how far the interest-based borrowings have contributed to the horrible inequalities found in our system of distribution, and how great is the injustice brought by the modern commercial interest to the whole society as compared to the interest charged on the old consumption loans that affected only some individuals.

168. How the present interest-based system works to favor the rich and kill the poor is succinctly explained by James Robertson in the following words:

"The pervasive role of interest in the economic system results in the systematic transfer of money from those who have less to those who have more. Again, this transfer of resources from poor to rich has been made shockingly clear by the Third World debt crisis. But it applies universally. It is partly because those who have more money to lend, get more in interest than those who have less; it is partly because those who have less, often have to borrow more; and it is partly because the cost of interest repayments now forms a substantial element in the cost of all goods and services, and the necessary goods and services looms much larger in the finances of the rich. When we look at the money system that way and when we begin to think about how it should be redesigned to carry out its functions fairly and efficiently as part of an enabling and conserving economy, the argument for an interest-free inflation-free money system for the twenty-first century seems to be very strong."

169. The same author in another book comments as follows:

"The transfer of revenue from poor people to rich people, from poor places to rich places, and from poor countries to rich countries by the money and finance system is systematic.... One cause of the transfer of wealth from poor to rich is the way interest payments and receipts work through the economy."

Back to Top

(d) Expansion of Artificial Money and Inflation

170. Since interest-bearing loans have no specific relation with actual production, and the financier, after securing a strong collateral, normally has no concern how the funds are used by the borrower, the money supply effected through banks and financial institutions has no nexus with the goods and services actually produced on the ground. It creates a serious mismatch between the supply of money and the production of goods and services. This is obviously one of the basic factors that create or fuel inflation.

171. This phenomenon is aggravated to a horrible extent by the well-known characteristic of the modern banks normally termed as "money creation." Even the introductory books of economics usually explain, often with complacence, how the banks create money. This apparently miraculous function of the banks is sometimes taken to be one of the factors that boost production and bring prosperity. But the illusion underlying this concept, is seldom unveiled by the champions of modern banking.

172. The history of "money creation" refers back to the famous story of the goldsmiths of medieval England. The people used to deposit their gold coins with them in trust, and they used to issue a receipt to the depositors. In order to simplify the process, the goldsmiths started issuing "bearer" receipts which gradually took the place of gold coins and the people started using them in settlement of their liabilities. When these receipts gained wide acceptability in the market, only a small fraction of the depositors or bearers ever came to the goldsmiths to demand actual gold. At this point the goldsmiths began lending out some of the deposited gold secretly and thus started earning interest on these loans. After some time they discovered that they could print more money (i.e. paper gold deposit certificates) than actually deposited with them and that they could loan out this extra money on interest. They acted accordingly and this was the birth of "money creation" or "fractional reserve lending" which means to loan out more money than one has as a reserve for deposits. In this way these goldsmiths, after becoming more confident, started decreasing the reserve requirement and increasing the percentage of their self-created credit, and used to loan out four, five, even ten times more gold certificates than they had in their safe rooms.

173. Initially, it was abuse of trust and a sheer fraud on the part of the goldsmiths not warranted by any norm of equity, justice and honesty. It was a form of forgery and usurpation of the power of the sovereign authority to issue money. But overtime, this fraudulent practice turned into the fashionable standard practice of the modern banks under the

"fractional reserve" system. How the money changers and bankers have succeeded in legalizing the creation of money by the private banks, in spite of the strong opposition from several rulers in England and USA, and how the Rothchilds acquired financial mastery over the whole of Europe and the Rockfeller over the whole of America is a long story, now lost in the mist of numerous theories developed to support the concept of money-creation by the private banks. But the net result is that the modern banks are creating money out of nothing. They are allowed to advance loans in the amounts ten times more than their deposits. The coins and notes issued by the government as a genuine and debt-free money have now a very insignificant proportion in the total money in circulation, most of which is artificial money created by advances made by the banks. The proportion of real money issued by the governments has been constantly declining in most of the countries, while the proportion of the artificial money created by the banks out of nothing is ever-increasing. The spiral of loans built upon loans is now the major part of the money supply. Taking the example of UK according to the statistics of 1997 the total money stock in the country was 680 billion pounds, out of which only 25 billion pounds were issued by the government in the form of coins and notes. All the rest i.e. 655 billion pounds were created by the banks. It means that the original debt-free money remained only 3.6% of the whole money supply while 96.4% is nothing but a bubble created by the banks. The way this bubble is growing annually can be seen from the following table that details the quantum of money supply in UK during twenty years:

Year	Total Coins and Notes issued by the Govt. (M0) S. Pound billion	TOTAL MONEY STOCK (M4) S. Pound bln.	Percentage of Real Debt-free Money to the Money Supply.
1977	8.1	65	12%
1979	10.5	87	12%
1981	12.1	116	10.5%
1983	12.8	161	7.9%
1985	14.1	205	6.8%
1987	15.5	269	5.8%
1989	17.2	372	4.6%
1991	18.6	485	3.8%
1993	20.0	525	3.8%
1995	22.4	585	3.8%
1997	25.0	680	3.6%

174. This table shows that the money created by the banks had been growing at a galloping speed throughout the two decades until it reached 680 billion pounds in 1997. The last column of the table shows the yearly declining percentage of the real money to the total money supply which fell from 12% in 1977 to 3.6% in 1997.

175. This phenomenon unveils two realities. Firstly, it shows that 96.4% of the total money supply is debt-ridden money and only 3.6% is debt-free. One can imagine how the whole economy is drowned under debt. Secondly, it means that 96.4% of the aggregate money circulated in the country is nothing but numbers created by computers, having no real thing behind them.

176. The situation in USA is almost the same as that in U.K. Patrick S.J. Carmack and Bill Still observe about it as follows:

> "Why are we over our head in debt? Because we are laboring under a debt-money system, in which all our money is created in parallel with an equivalent quantity of debt, that is designed and controlled by private bankers for their benefit. They create and loan money at interest, we get the debt...
>
> ...So, although the banks do not create currency, they do create checkbook money, or deposits, by making new loans. They even invest some of this created money. In fact, over one trillion dollars of this privately-created money has been used to purchase U.S. bonds on the open market, which provides the banks with roughly 50 billion dollars in interest, less the interest they pay some depositors. In this way, through fractional reserve lending, banks create far in excess of 90% of the money, and therefore cause over 90% of our inflation."

177. Although the conventional Quantity theory of money has suggested many devices to control the money supply, including the control of interest rates by the government, these remedies are not the cure of the disease. They are temporary measures and

they themselves have their own side effects that subject the economy with shocks of the business cycle. Michael Rowbotham has rightly observed:

> "This (monetary management) a government does by lowering or raising interest rates. This alternately encourages or discourages borrowing, thereby speeding up or slowing down the creation of money and the growth of the economy.... The fact that, by this method, people and businesses with outstanding debts can be suddenly hit with huge extra charges on their debts, simply as a management device to deter other borrowers, is an injustice quite lost in the almost religious conviction surrounding this ideology...
>
> ...This method of controlling banks, inflation and money supply certainly works; it works in the way that a sledge-hammer works at carving up a roast chicken. An economy dependent upon borrowing to supply money, strapped to a financial system in which both debt and the money supply are logically bound to escalate, is punished for the borrowing it has been forced to undertake. Many past borrowers are rendered bankrupt; homes are repossessed, businesses are ruined and millions are thrown out of work

as the economy sinks into recession. Until inflation and overheating are no longer deemed to be a danger, borrowing is discouraged and the economy becomes a stagnating sea of human misery. Of course, no sooner has this been done, than the problem is lack of demand, so we must reduce interest rates and wait for the consumer confidence and the positive investment climate to return. The business cycle begins all over again - There could be no greater admission of the utter and total inadequacy of modern economics to understand and regulate the financial system than through this wholesale entrapment and subsequent bludgeoning of the entire economy. It is a policy which courts illegality, as well as breaching morality, in the cavalier way in which the financial contract of debt is effectively rewritten at will, via the power of levying infinitely variable interest charges."

178. Moreover, the baseless money created by the banks and financial institutions itself has now become the subject of speculative trade through the derivatives in the form of Futures and Options in the international markets. What it means is that in the beginning, claims over money have been treated as money. Now, claims over claims are being treated as such. According to an estimate, over 150 trillion US dollars worth of derivatives are

circulating in the world, whereas the combined GDP of all the 188 countries of the world is around 30 trillion US dollars only. Almost 80% of this trade is in the hands of some two dozen big banks and hedge funds. The whole economy of the world has thus been turned into a big balloon that is being inflated on daily basis by new debts and new financial transactions having no nexus whatsoever with the real economy. This big balloon is vulnerable to the market shocks and can be burst any time. It really did several times in the recent past whereby the Asian Tigers reached the brink of total collapse, and the effects of these shocks were felt in the whole world to the extent that the media started crying that the market economy is breathing its last. Once again, we would like to quote James Robertson, who in his excellent work 'Transforming Economic Life: A Millennial Challenge" has commented on this aspect as follows:

> "The money-must-grow imperative is ecologically destructive... (It) also results in a massive world-wide diversion of effort away from providing useful goods and services, into making money out of money. At least 954b of the billions of dollars transferred daily around the world are of purely financial transactions, unlinked to transactions in the real economy.
>
> People are increasingly experiencing the workings of the money, banking and finance system as unreal, incomprehensible, unaccountable,

irresponsible, exploitative and out of control. Why should they lose their houses and their jobs as a result of financial decisions taken in distant parts of the world? Why should the national and international money and finance system involve the systematic transfer of wealth from poor people to rich people, and from poor countries to rich countries? Why someone in Singapore be able to gamble on Tokyo Stock Exchange and bring about the collapse of a bank in London? ... Why do young people trading in derivatives in the City of London get annual bonuses larger than the whole annual budgets of primary school? Do we have to have a money and financial system that works like this? Even the financier George Sores has said ("Capital Crimes", Atlantic Monthly, January, 1997) that "the untrammeled intensification of laissez-faire capitalism and the extension of market values into all areas of life is endangering our open and democratic society. The main enemy of the open society, I believe, is no longer the Communist but the Capitalist Threat."

179. All this appalling situation faced by the whole world today is the logical outcome of giving the interest-based financial system an unbridled power to reign the economy. Can one still insist that the

commercial interest is an innocent transaction? In fact the universal horrors brought about by the commercial interest are far greater than the individual usurious loans that used to affect only some individuals.

My Comments 17: **The learned Judge has again made Interest the scapegoat for the appalling situation. This situation is, in fact, the logical outcome of giving the *Ar-Riba*-based financial system an unbridled power to reign the economy! In other words, the financial system has been reduced to this sorry state, not because it is interest-based, but because it is *Ar-Riba*-based! This is the truth that comes out distinctly if we analyse the position statements and the expert opinions closely.**

The appalling situation was created not because the banks took honest inerest on money lent by them out of the funds they actually had. It was because the quantum of the money they lent out was more than the quantum they actually had. They had created a fraud by lending money which never was! They were not therefore legally or morally entitled to the interest they took on the baseless money. They thus enriched themselves with other people's money, i.e. 'fee amwaalinnasi' in the terminology of the Qur'aan. They thus committed 'Ar-Riba', in the light of verse 30.39!

The financial system came to this sorry pass not because the financial institutions were interest-based. It was because the system permitted the institutions to resort to gambling and speculation

in the equity market. In my comments under paragraph 152 above, I have shown why the quick buck, the institutions thus got, was pure *Ar-Riba!*

Back to Top

Interest and Indexation

180, Some appellants have tried to justify the interest charged and paid by the banks on the ground that since the value of money is decreasing constantly, the interest should be taken as a compensation for the erosion of the value of money during the period of borrowing. The financier, according to them, should have a right to claim at least the same amount in real terms as he had advanced to the borrower, but if his principal is repaid to him in the same numerical terms, he will not receive the same purchasing power as he had advanced to his debtor, because the inflation would have eroded a substantial part of the real value of money. Therefore, they argue, the interest is paid to compensate the loss the financier has suffered through inflation.

181. This argument is without force because the rates of interest are though a major cause of inflation among other factors, they are not based on the rate of inflation. Had it been compensation for inflation, the rate of interest should have always matched the rate of inflation, and obviously this is not the case. The rates of interest are determined by the demand and supply of money and not by the rate of inflation at the time of the contract. If at any

given time both rates match each other, it may be by chance and not as a matter of principle. Therefore, the interest cannot be held as a compensation for the loss of purchasing power.

182. Some other quarters have taken the aspect of inflation from another angle. They do not claim that interest, as in vogue, is a compensation for the loss caused by inflation. However, they suggest that indexation of loans can be a suitable substitute for the present interest bearing loans. They argue that the financier should be compensated for the erosion of the value of money he had advanced to the borrower and therefore he can claim an additional amount matching the rate of inflation. Thus, according to them, indexation may be introduced into the banking system as an alternative for interest.

183. But without going into the question whether indexation of loans are or are not in conformity with Shar'iah, this suggestion is not practical so far as the banking transactions are concerned. The reason is obvious. The concept of indexation of loans is to give the real value of the principal to the financier based on the rate of inflation, and therefore, there is no difference between depositors and borrowers in this respect. It means that the bank will receive from its borrowers the same rate as it will have to pay to its depositors, both being based on the same measure i.e. the rate of inflation. Thus nothing will be left for the banks themselves, and no bank can be run without a profit. Mr. Khalid M. Ishaq, advocate, who seemed to be inclined towards indexation, was asked by the bench how the banking system can be established on the basis of indexation alone. He

frankly admitted that he had no ready answer, but the suggestion should be considered in depth. Some bankers who appeared to assist the court, especially Mr. Abdul Jabbar Khan, the former President of the National Bank of Pakistan, gave his absolute opinion that the suggestion of taking indexation as a substitute of interest is not practicable from banking point of view.

184. It is clear from this discussion that neither the present interest rates can be justified on the basis of inflation, nor can indexation be used as a substitute for interest in the present banking system.

185. However, the question of erosion of the value of money is certainly relevant to the individual loans and unpaid debts. There are many cases where the creditors really face hardships, especially where the value of the currency fell to an unimaginable extent, as happened in Turkey, Syria, Lebanon and in the States of the former Soviet Union. In our country too, the value of the rupee today is much less than it was before 1970. The question is whether a person who has advanced a sum of Rs.1000/-before 1970 and the debtor did not pay the principal till today is entitled to get the same Rs.1000/-, while this amount has remained not more than Rs.100/- in real terms? This question is more severe where the debtor did not pay despite his being able to pay.

186. In order to solve this problem, many suggestions have been proposed by different quarters, some of which are the following:

a) That the loans should be indexed, meaning thereby, that the debtor must pay an additional amount equal to the increase in the rate of inflation during the period of borrowing.

b) That the loans should be tied up with gold, and it should be presumed that the one who has loaned Rs.1000/- has actually loaned as much gold as could be purchased on that date for Rs.1000/- and must repay as much rupees as are sufficient to purchase that much of gold.

c) That the loans should be tied up by a hard currency like dollar.

d) That the loss of the value of money should be shared by both creditor and lender in equal proportion. If the value of money has declined at a ratio of 5%, 2.5% should be paid by the debtor and the rest should be borne by the creditor, because the inflation is a phenomenon beyond the control of either of them. Being a common suffering, both should share it.

187. But we feel that this question needs a more thorough research which before its final decision in this Court should first be initiated by different study circles of the country, especially, by the Council of Islamic Ideology and the Commission for the

Islamization of Economy. Many international seminars have been held to deliberate on this issue. The papers and resolutions of these seminars should be analyzed in depth.

188. On the other hand, having held that this question does neither justify interest nor provides a substitute for it in the banking transactions, we do not have to resolve this issue in this case, nor does the decision about the laws under challenge depend on it. We, therefore, leave the question open for further study and research.

My Comments 18: **The learned Judge did show some grasp of reality in considering this aspect of the matter. How could the banks run if they are not compensated for the erosion in the value of money lent? How, indeed!**

But the learned Judge still maintained that inflation did not justify taking of interest by the banks! The position taken by him is that on no account is taking of interest justified. How then could the banks meet their huge legitimate expenses?

In order to meet these expenses, it appears, the Judge would like the banks to invest in the equity market on the profit/loss sharing basis. They could thus provide the finance needed by commercial and industrial concerns, and also get their share of the profits made by the concerns to meet their (the banks') own expenses.

Well and good! But the obvious catch is: what if the equity market is completely down as at

present (2001-2002)? The banks would have only losses to bear and no profit!

To obviate such an eventuality the banks resort to a judicious mix of investments in both the debt and equity markets. But the learned Judge would not like the banks to have anything to do with interest!

The Truth is that the Judge has made a lamentable mistake in holding that Islam prohibits interest. He failed to see that *Ar-Riba,*which Allah forbids, covers all economic injustices (like the ones discussed herein above in his Judgement), and not interest as such!

The Qur'aan provides a solutuion to the inflation problem too! In verse 2.279, it says that the lender is entitled to his 'amwaal'. Money is actually not 'amwaal'. It is only the current value of 'amwaal'. Therefore, when I deposit $1000 in a bank today, it is as if I am depositing goods ('amwaal') of the current value of $1000. One year hence, the divine law requires that I get back the same 'amwaal'. If the current value of the goods were to increase to $1100 in the meantime, the bank would have to give me $1100.

It is thus clear that the divine law requires that inflation should be taken into account while returning money to either the depositor or the lender. This is besides 'interest' which a bank may also be entitled to, under this head of its rightful 'amwaal'.

There is no need to panic. Both the interest rates and the inflation rates are bound to come down drastically, once the injunction on the real 'Ar-Riba' is implemented honestly.

Back to Top

Mark-up and Interest

189. Some appellants have argued that although the interest is prohibited by the Holy Qur'an and Sunnah, the present banks do not deal in interest. Instead, they charge mark-up from their customers. Mr Haafiz S.A. Rahman, the learned counsel for the Agricultural Development Bank of Pakistan gave a detailed history of the legal steps taken by the government of Pakistan to eliminate interest from its economy. According to him, effective 1 April 1998, all types of finance to all types of clients including individuals were obligated to be designed on interest-free basis. On 1 July 1995 interest bearing deposits ceased to be accepted and the deposits were ordered to be based on PLS (profit and loss sharing) basis except the current accounts which do not attract any return. In order to implement this directive, the State Bank of Pakistan allowed 12 modes of financing, all free of interest, for the banks and financial institutions. The government has also brought amendments to a large number of financial laws to eliminate interest from the economy. After all these steps are taken, interest is no more applicable in the banking transactions of the country. All the banks today are working under 12 modes of financing announced by the State Bank of Pakistan. The appellants argued that since the

interest has already been abolished, the Respondents have no reason to pray for elimination of interest.

190. The history given by Haafiz S.A. Rahman is essentially true and it is correct that the State Bank of Pakistan had suggested 12 modes of financing instead of interest, but the practical situation on the ground is that out of all these 12 modes only 2 or 3 modes are normally being used by the banks and financial institutions, the foremost among them being mark-up. But the way the mark-up is used by the banks today is nothing but a change of nomenclature of the transaction. Practically what is being done is to replace the name of interest by the name of mark-up. The concept of mark-up was originally presented by the Council of Islamic Ideology in its report on the Elimination of *Riba* submitted to the government of Pakistan in 1980. The Council has in fact suggested that the true alternative to the interest is profit and loss sharing (PLS) based on Musharakah and Mudarabah. However, there were some areas in which financing on the basis of Musharakah and Mudarabah were not practicable. For these areas the Council has suggested a technique usually known in the Islamic banks as Murabahah. According to this technique the financier bank, instead of advancing a loan in the form of money, purchases the commodity required by the customers from the market and then sells it to the customer on deferred payment basis retaining a margin of mark-up (profit) added to its cost. It was not a financing in its strict sense. It was rather a sale of a commodity effected in favor of the client. The very concept of this transaction implies the following points:

a) This type of transaction may be undertaken only where the client of a bank wants to purchase a commodity. This type of transaction cannot be effected in cases where the client wants to get funds for some purpose other than purchasing a commodity, like overhead expenses, payment of salaries, settlement of bills or other liabilities.

b) To make it a valid transaction it was necessary that the commodity is really purchased by the bank and it comes into the ownership and possession (physical or constructive) of the bank so that it may assume the risk of the commodity so far as it remains under its ownership and possession.

c) After acquiring the ownership and possession of the commodity it should be sold to the customer through a valid sale.

d) The Council has also suggested that this device should be used to the minimum extent only in cases where Musharakah or Mudarabah are not practicable for one reason or another.

191. Unfortunately, while implementing this technique by the banks and the financial institutions, all the above points were totally ignored. What was done was to change the name of

interest and replace it by the name of mark-up. The mark-up system as in vogue today has no concern with any real commodity whatsoever. In most cases there is no commodity at all in real sense; if there is any, it is never purchased by the banks nor sold to the customers after acquiring it. In some cases this technique is applied on the basis of buy-back arrangement which means that the commodity already owned by the customer is sold by him to the bank and is simultaneously purchased by him from the bank at a higher price which is nothing but to make fun of the original concept. In many cases it is done merely on papers without a genuine commodity to be sold and purchased. Moreover, this technique is applied indiscriminately to all the banking transactions having no regard whether or not they involve a commodity. The procedure is being applied to all types of finances including financing overhead expenses, payment of bills etc. The net result is that no meaningful change has ever been brought about to the system of interest on the assets side of the banks. Therefore, all the objections against interest are very much applicable to the mark-up system as in vogue in Pakistan and this system cannot be held as immune from being declared as repugnant to the Holy Qur'an and Sunnah. We hold accordingly.

<u>My Comments 19</u>: The learned Judge's description of the position prevailing in Pakistan is an admission that the so-called Islamic alternative modes adopted to avoid interest are impracticable and therefore liable to be reduced to taking Interest itself, but under a different name.

Seeking the alternatives to Interest is an unncessary futile exercise, since Islam does not prohibit Interest, *per se.*

Back to Top

Qarz and Qiraz

192. Dr. M. Aslam Khaki, the appellant in Shariat Appeal No.1 (S) 1992 was not a party to the proceedings in the Federal Shariat Court in these cases. However, the matter being of general importance we heard him at length. In the memo of his appeal he had adopted almost the same lines of argument as we have already dealt with but while appearing in the court his arguments were on totally different lines. He expressed his opinion that if the financing transaction stipulates a fixed return to the financier regardless of whether the financed party has gained a profit or suffered a loss, it should be regarded as *riba*. But if the financing transaction contemplates that in the case of a loss, the loss will be shared by both the parties in proportion to their respective investments, this much is enough to validate the transaction after which the parties can agree on a condition that if the business gains a profit a certain rate of profit attributable to the original investment of the financier will be deserved by him. It will become a transaction of Qiraz which is not impermissible in Shar'iah.

193. At the first place, this standpoint does not save the laws under consideration from the attack of the Respondents because these laws ensure a fixed return to the financier in any case, therefore, his appeal, to save the said laws from being declared as

repugnant to the injunctions of Islam, is misconceived. His standpoint can be considered only in the context of finding out alternatives to the interest in our banking system. But his view is not supported by the Holy Qur'an and Sunnah, nor by any jurist throughout the fourteen centuries. Qiraz is a term used in the literature of the Islamic Fiqh as a synonym to Mudarabah and all the schools of Islamic Fiqh are unanimous on the point that in an agreement of Mudarabah no rate of profit attributable to the investment can be allocated for the financier. Any such arrangement has been held by the jurists as impermissible. The standpoint of the appellant is contradictory in itself because he admits that in the case of loss, the financier does not deserve any profit but on the other hand if the financier has stipulated 10% of his investment as his share in the profit of the business, it is acceptable to the appellant. But what will happen if the whole profit is not more than 10%. In this case the whole profit according to him will be secured by the financier and the Mudarib will get nothing, despite the business having earned a profit. This view is, therefore, fallacious on the face of it.

My Comments: Please see my comments under paragraph 191 above.

Back to Top

Riba and Doctrine of Necessity

194. Lastly, some appellants have tried to attract the doctrine of necessity to the case of *riba*. Mr. Siddiq AlFarooq, the Managing Director of House Building Finance Corporation (HBFC) argued that

the Holy Qur'an has allowed even to eat pork in the case of extreme hunger to save one's life. The argument of some appellant was that the interest-based system has now become a universal necessity and no country can live without it. Interest is no doubt prohibited by the Holy Qur'an but to implement this prohibition on countrywide level may be a suicidal act which may shatter the whole economy, therefore, it should not be declared as repugnant to the injunctions of Islam. Some appellants have argued that the whole world today is turning into a global village and no country can survive in seclusion, especially, our country which is drowned in debts and its most development projects depend chiefly on the foreign loans based on interest. Once the prohibition of interest is enforced at a whole-sale basis all the development projects will breath their last and the whole economy will face a sudden collapse.

195. We have given due attention to this line of argument and examined this aspect seriously with the assistance of a number of economists, bankers and professional practitioners. No doubt, Islam is a realistic religion and it never binds an individual or a State with a command, the implementation of which is beyond its control. The doctrine of necessity is one of the doctrines enshrined and developed by the Holy Qur'an and Sunnah and expounded by the Muslim jurists. It is rightly pointed out by Mr. Siddiq AlFarooq that the Holy Qur'an has allowed even to eat pork in a case of extreme hunger where the life of a human being cannot be saved without it. But the doctrine of necessity in Islam is not an obscure concept. There are certain criteria expounded by the Muslim jurists

in the light of the Holy Qur'an and Sunnah to determine the magnitude of necessity and the extent to which a Qur'anic command can be relaxed on the basis of an emergent situation. Therefore, before deciding an issue on the basis of necessity one must make sure that the necessity is real and not exaggerated by imaginary apprehensions and that the necessity cannot be met with by any other means than committing an impermissible act. When we analyze the case of interest in the light of the above principles we are of the firm view that there is a great deal of exaggeration in the apprehension that the elimination of interest will lead the economy to collapse. For a realistic analysis we will have to consider the domestic transactions and the foreign transactions separately.

Back to Top

Domestic Transactions

196. In the domestic transactions the apprehension against the elimination of interest is often based on some misconceptions. There are many people who think that abolishing interest means to turn the banks into charitable institutions and that the banks, in an Islamic system, will advance money with no return and the depositors will get nothing on their money held in the banks. Obviously, this misconception is based on sheer ignorance of the Islamic principles. We have already discussed at length the concept of a Loan in Islam and that its role in the commercial economy is very limited. What is meant by Islamizing the banks and financial institutions is not to advance money without return; what it does mean is that the banks will finance on

the basis of profit and loss sharing, and other Islamic modes of financing, none of which is devoid of return.

197. Some other people are of the view that the alternative banking system based on Islamic principles has not yet been designed nor practiced, and therefore, by implementing it abruptly we will enter into a dark and obscure area and subject ourselves to unseen dangers that may bring total disaster to our economy.

198. This apprehension is also based on unawareness of the new thoughts about the present financial system and about what has been happening in the field of Islamic banking for the last three decades. The fact is that Islamic banking is no longer a fanciful or utopian dream. Muslim jurists and economists have been working on various aspects of Islamic banking from different dimensions for the last 50 years, and it is from the 1970s that the concept of Islamic banks has been translated into real institutions working on the Islamic lines. The number of Islamic banks and financial institutions throughout the world has been growing during the last 3 decades. As stated by Mr. Iqbal Ahmad Khan, the head of the Islamic banking division of HSBC London who appeared in this case as a juris-consult, the number of Islamic banks and financial institutions has now reached more than 200 across 65 countries of the world with US $90 billion capital at a growth rate of 15% p.a. By the year 2000 the Islamic Finance Industry is expected to be a US $100 billion plus business.

199. The present Islamic Development Bank (IDB) based in Jeddah was established in 1975 by the Organization of Islamic Conference (OIC) as a pioneer of Islamic banking. This bank was originally meant for inter-governmental financial transactions providing funds for development projects in the member countries. But it is now providing trade finance facilities to the private sector also. This bank has its own research center working on different issues of Islamic banking and economy. The Court invited this bank to send some of its experts to assist the Court and to throw light on the working of the Islamic banks and the feasibility of the proposals presented so far for transforming the banking system to the Islamic ways of financing. The bank was kind enough to send a high level delegation headed by the President of the Bank Dr. Ahmad Muhammad Afi himself. Several members of the delegation, including the President of the Bank, addressed the Court and have submitted their report in writing. Details apart, the substance of their submissions is summarized in their own words as follows:

> "The experience accumulated by Islamic banks, in general, and the Islamic Development Bank in particular, as well as attempts made in a number of Muslim countries to apply an Islamic financial system, indicate that the application of such an Islamic system by any Muslim country, at the national level, is feasible. According to the data compiled by the International Union of Islamic Banks, there are 176

Islamic banks and institutions in the world. In terms of number, 47% of these institutions are concentrated in South and south East Asia, 27% in GCC and Middle East, 20% in Africa and 6% in the Western countries. In terms of deposits, amounting to US $112.6 billion and total assets amounting to US $147.7 billion. 73% of the activities of these institutions are concentrated in the GCC and the Middle East. IDB alone, since its inception from 1976 to 1999, has provided financing in the range of US $21.0 billion. As against a growth rate of 7% per annum recorded by the global financial services industry, Islamic banking is growing at a rate of 10-15% per annum and accounts for 50-60% of the share of the market in the GCC and Middle East."

"Islamic banking is distinctive in two respects: concentrating on the real sector of the economy, it imparts tremendous stability to the economic system by achieving an identity between monetary flows and goods and services, and by operating on a system of profit and loss sharing in its evolved state, it insulates the society from the debt-mountain on the analogy that if the economies enter into recessionary or deflationary phases, the principles of profit and loss sharing protects the states and economic operators from the evils of accumulation of interest and minimizes defaults and bankruptcies."

200. Since the experience of Islamic banking is passing through its initial phase, the industry is facing numerous issues. These issues have given birth to a number of research institutes, study circles, training programs and specialized groups. There is a large number of seminars, workshops and conferences, held every year in different parts of the world where the Muslim jurists, economists, bankers and practitioners sort out the practical problems and find out their solutions.

201. This does never mean that the Islamic banking industry has achieved the ultimate goal of its maturity. It certainly has its limitations. It may be suffering from a number of weaknesses. There are many issues yet to be resolved. But the progress made by the Islamic banks so far is sufficient to refute the misconception that it is a utopian idea, or that any advance in this direction will make us step into a void. This brief account does at least show that much of the ground work has been done in the field of Islamic banking, and while discussing the possibilities of the elimination of interest from the economy, this background cannot be ignored or undervalued.

202. Mr. M. Ashraf Janjua, the Chief Economic Advisor of the State Bank of Pakistan, has been nominated by the SEP as its representative during the hearing of this case. In his written statement

submitted to the Court he has opined that shifting of the entire interest-based system to one that is free from interest is feasible, but it is a more complex and challenging task than the one undertaken by the private Islamic banks working in different part of the world.

203. We are not unconscious of the fact that elimination of interest from the entire economy is more complex and challenging in many respects than abolishing it from a single institution. But at the same time, there are many areas where establishing an interest-free system is much easier for the government than it was for the private Islamic banks. The Islamic banks working in different parts of the world do not enjoy any support from their respective governments or the central banks for their interest-free transactions. They have to submit to the legal framework and the regulatory requirements that are basically designed for interest-based financing, but are imposed on the Islamic banks with the same force without the slightest change in favor of Islamic modes of financing. The Islamic banks are working with their hands tied by the conventional laws and regulations. If the interest-free system is introduced by the government itself at country level, the government will be free to bring its own legal and regulatory framework and the difficulties faced by the private Islamic banks will create no problem for the government. Moreover, the Islamic banks have to compete with the conventional banks. Any client not happy with the arrangement offered by the Islamic banks can easily go to a conventional bank, the other alternative being readily available. If the Islamic modes are enforced at country level, and no

bank offers an interest-based arrangement, this problem can easily be overcome. The correct position, therefore, is that abolishing interest at country level is easier in some respects and more difficult in some others. To be realistic, we should realize both aspects while determining the time frame for conversion. Let us now examine the main features of the proposed system of Islamic banking.

Back to Top

Profit and Loss Sharing

204. The basic and foremost characteristic of Islamic financing is that, instead of a fixed rate of interest, it is based on profit and loss sharing. We have already discussed the horrible results produced by the debt-based economy. Realizing the evils brought by this system, many economists, even of the Western world are now advocating in favor of an equity-based financial arrangement. To quote James Robertson again:

> "Why has the process of issuing new money into economy (i.e. credit creation) been delegated by governments to the banks, allowing them to profit from issuing it in the form of interest-bearing loans to their customers? Should governments not issue it directly themselves, as a component of a citizen's income?"

> "Would it be desirable and possible to limit the role of interest more

> drastically than that, for example by converting debt into equity throughout the economy? This would be in line with Islamic teaching, and with earlier Christian teaching, that usury is sin. Although the practical complications would make this a goal for the longer term, there are strong arguments for exploring it - the extent to which economic life world-wide now depends on ever-rising debt, the danger of economic collapse this entails, and the economic power now enjoyed by those who make money out of money rather than out of risk-bearing participation in useful enterprises."

205. John Tomlinson is an Oxford based Canadian economist. Having studied the effect of debt on the economies of developed and less developed countries, he set up and is the Chairman of Oxford Research and Development Corporation Limited which explores the use of equity instruments and the development of equity markets for areas of finance currently served by debt. In his book "Honest Money" he has strongly recommended the conversion of debt into equity. His following conclusions merit consideration for those who are adamant on maintaining status quo in the financial system:

> "Converting debt to equity is not a panacea for all economic ills. It can, however, produce many positive benefits. These benefits will not

necessarily follow automatically from conversion. Concentrated effort will be required to ensure they do. Without conversion they will not happen at all.

Not the least of these benefits will be those brought to the banking community itself. The banking and monetary system will not collapse. Nor should there ever need to be the threat of collapse again. Owners of banks will find the value of their shares underpinned as liabilities disappear from balance sheets and are replaced by assets of a specific value. Each and every depositor will be able simultaneously to withdraw his or her total deposits.

Demand for the bank's current or cheque account services will not diminish. Longer term depositors will now have to pay for storage: it will be a less attractive option than exchange, so the velocity with which money moves from bank to market-place to bank again, from one account to another, is likely to increase. There will be a continuous flow of money available for new equity investment.

The market-place in general will also receive benefits. Conversion will also cause the value of money to stabilize. Savings can then retain their value. Prices need only vary according to the supply and demand of the product being priced. Measurements of exchange value made by different people at different times can be validly compared. The unit of money will once more be a valid unit of measurement of exchange value. The field of economics can become a science.

Many of the distortions which now exist in our individual frames of reference will be corrected. For instance, an investment which took an investor, ten, fifteen or twenty years to recoup used to be considered sound. Now, too often the maximum period envisaged is five years; even three. This short-term view has precluded many useful businesses from being created. The re-establishment of stable money and the emphasis on security which will be required within equity investment program will encourage people to take a longer view. More businesses will then be considered viable and the number of new jobs can increase dramatically.

Existing savers will also be protected. The conversion to equity will eliminate the possibility of collapse for individual banks and for the system as a whole. Savings will not disappear. The nature of savings will change from just units of money to units of money and shares. The exchange value of both the shares and the money will have to be re-assessed. But they will have value. If no actions is taken and the system collapses, they may end up having no value.

The changes proposed will also free many from the enslavement of debt. Both nations and individuals can regain their dignity. They will be free to make their own choices. No longer will managers have to face the choice between paying interest and disemploying some or not paying interest and disemploying all.

Nor shall we need to experience the stresses caused by current economic and business cycles. There will be a steady flow of money into investments. New investment opportunities will continually be sought as a home for both individual saving and business profits. Both will wish to avoid storage charges.

Growth will be dependent upon the continuing development of new ideas and new productive capacity. Growth will no longer be dependent upon the creation of new debt.

Economic expansion will depend upon the positive flow of new savings and new profits.

Re-establishing the integrity of money will eliminate at least one of the causes of human conflict. Money will no longer secretly steal from those who save, those on fixed income and those who enter long-term contracts.

Further, it can lead to a greater premium being placed on personal integrity. The character traits of honest, honorable and forthright behavior will be in demand. Investors' security will depend on them. Recognition of the degree of interdependence in an equity-oriented market-place can lead to more consideration of the needs of others, and, ultimately, to a more caring and, compassionate society.

Of course, life is never roses all the way. Many mistakes will be made. When new paths are trodden, the way is sometimes uncertain. Some will find it difficult to break the habitual patterns of thought which govern behavior in a debt-oriented society. No doubt some readers will have already experienced this.

Some will be hard-pressed when the actual exchange value of their investments becomes apparent. Yet, the conversion process can be controlled. Collapse cannot. We should be able, as part of the conversion process, to identify those who might suffer unduly. Then we can be prepared to assist them and cushion any hardship. The case of honest money is a compelling one. Honest money is not a thief. It does not steal from the thrifty. It is not socially divisive. It does not promote economic and business cycles, creating unemployment. On the contrary, it encourages thrift. It promotes sustainable economic growth. It rewards merit. It demands integrity. These were worthwhile goals. They can be achieved. What is needed now is the will to make them happen."

206. Michael Rowbotham has commented on the above-quoted book of Tomlinson as follows:

"One of the most unusual and original contributions to the monetary debate. John Tomlinson is a former merchant banker and presents a powerful case against the debt-based money system; his solution is highly creative and shows the scope for thought outside the normal parameters of monetary reform. The work is currently being incorporated by Nova University in America as part of their master degree in economics."

207. Philip Moore, in his recent study of Islamic Finance, observes as follows:

> "Although this long term shift from a bond-based to an equity-based financial system accords in many respects with Islamic economic principles, it is a trend which is by no means confined to the Islamic world and which is increasingly being championed globally. The resurgence in Islamic finance worldwide is seen by some simply as a reflection of the global economy's discernible transition from bond-based to equity-based finance.
>
> Consider, for example, the strategy of a developed, non-Muslim but heavily indebted economy such as Italy. Under the terms of privatization programme which gathered momentum in 1995 and 1996, Italian law stipulates that ".....all the proceeds of the privatization of public companies become part of a sinking fund that, by law, can only be used to retire debt, and is not applied towards the reduction of the PSBR." Perhaps, indeed, the Western world has been

gravitating towards Islamic principles of finance without knowing it over the last three decades."

208. Mr. Abbes Mirakhor and Mohsin H. Khan, both economists of the Research Department of the International Monetary Fund (IMF) have studied in detail the implications of an interest-free Islamic banking, and while discussing the profit and loss system they have observed:

> "As shown in a recent paper by Khan (1985) this system of investment deposits is quite closely related to proposals aimed at transforming the traditional banking system to an equity basis made frequently in a number of countries, including the United States."

Peter Warburton has also preferred an equity-based financial system and has discussed the theories of Fisher, Minsky, J. Presley and P. Mills in this respect.

209. Thus, the equity-based banking is not something proposed by the Islamic circles alone. It is being suggested also by some non-Muslim economists on purely economic grounds. The injustice, instability and business shocks created by the present debt-based financial system have themselves compelled them to think about an equity-based system that has more potential to bring about distributive justice and stability. In equity-based banking the depositors are expected to gain

much more than they are receiving today in the form of interest which often becomes negative in real terms by the inflation caused mainly by the expansion of the debt-based money. It will divert the flow of wealth towards the common people and in turn will encourage savings and bring a gradual and balanced prosperity.

Back to Top

Some Objections on Musharakah Financing

1. Risk of Loss

210. It is argued that the arrangement of Musharakah is more likely to pass on losses of the business to the financier bank or institution. This loss will be passed on to depositors also. The depositors, being constantly exposed to the risk of loss, will not like to deposit their money in the banks and financial institutions and thus their savings will either remain idle or will be used in transactions outside the banking channels, which will not contribute to the economic development at national level.

211. This argument is, however, misconceived. Before financing on the basis of Musharakah, the banks and financial institution will study the feasibility of the proposed business for which funds are needed. Even in the present system of interest-based loans the banks do not advance loans to each and every applicant. They study not only the financial position of the client, but in some cases they have to examine the potentials of the business and if they apprehend that the business is not

profitable, they refuse to advance a loan. In the case of Musharakah, they will have to carry out this study at a wider scale with more depth and precaution, but this extra work will certainly contribute a lot to the betterment of the economy as a whole.

212. Moreover, no bank or financial institution can restrict itself to a single Musharakah. There will always be a diversified portfolio of Musharakah. If a bank has financed 100 of its clients on the basis of Musharakah, after studying the feasibility of the proposal of each one of them, it is hardly conceivable that all of these Musharakahs, or the majority of them will result in a loss. After taking proper measures and due care, what can happen at the most is that some of them make a loss. But on the other hand, the profitable Musharakahs are expected to give more return than the interest-based loans, because the actual profit is supposed to be distributed between the client and the bank. Therefore, the Musharakah portfolio, as a whole, is not expected to suffer loss, and the possibility of loss to the whole portfolio is merely a theoretical possibility which should not discourage the depositors. This theoretical possibility of loss in a financial institution is much less than the possibility of loss in a joint stock company whose business is restricted to a limited sector of commercial activities. Still, the people purchase its shares and the possibility of loss does not refrain them from investing in these shares. The case of the bank and financial institutions is much stronger, because their Musharakah activities will be so diversified that any possible loss in one Musharakah is expected to be more than compensated by the profits earned in

other Musherakahs. The experience of Pakistani banks is an empirical evidence. Since 1 July 1995 all the deposits in Pakistan are based on profit and loss sharing basis, except current account. No guarantee even of the principal, is provided to the depositors by the banks, and thus the liabilities side of our present banks is fully equity-based. Still, the deposits are being made as before.

213. Apart from this, an Islamic economy must create a mentality which believes that any profit earned on money is the reward of bearing risks of the business. This risk may be minimized through expertise and diversifying the portfolio where it may become a hypothetical or theoretical risk only. But there is no way to eliminate this risk totally. The one who wants to earn profit, must accept this minimal risk. Since this understanding is already there in the case of normal joint stock companies, nobody has ever raised the objection that the money of the shareholders is exposed to loss. The problem is created by the system that separates the banking and financing from the normal trade activities, and which has compelled the people to believe that banks and financial institutions deal in money and papers only, and that they have nothing to do with the actual results emerging in trade and industry. It is this basic premise on the basis of which it is argued that they deserve a fixed return in any case. This essential separation of financing sector from the sector of trade and industry has brought great harms to the economy at macro-level. Obviously, when we speak of Islamic banking, we never mean that it will follow this conventional system in each and every respect. Islam has its own values and principles which do not believe in separation of

financing from trade and industry. Once this Islamic system is understood, the people will invest in the financing sector, despite the theoretical risk of loss, more readily than they invest in the profitable joint stock companies.

Back to Top

2. Dishonesty

214. Another apprehension against Musharakah financing is that the dishonest clients may exploit the instrument of Musharakah by not paying any return to the financiers. They can always show that the business did not earn any profit. Indeed, they can claim that it has suffered a loss in which case not only the profit, but also the principal amount will be jeopardized.

215. It is, no doubt, a valid apprehension, especially in societies where corruption is the order of the day. However, solution to this problem is not as difficult as is generally believed or exaggerated.

216. If all the banks in a country are run on pure Islamic pattern with a careful support from the Central Bank and the government, the problem of dishonesty is not hard to overcome. First of all, the system of credit rating will have to be implemented with full force. Every company or corporate body should be compelled by law to subject itself to an independent credit rating. Even the big firms seeking finance above a certain level may also be subjected to the same rule. Secondly, a well-designed system of auditing should be implemented whereby the accounts of all the clients are fully

maintained and properly controlled. According to some contemporary scholars, profits may be calculated on the basis of gross margins only. It will reduce the possibility of disputes and misappropriation. However, if any misconduct, dishonesty or negligence is established against a client, he will be subjected to punitive steps, and may be deprived of availing any facility from any bank in the country, at least for a specific period.

217. These steps will serve as strong deterrent against concealing the actual profits or committing any other act of dishonesty. Otherwise also, the clients of the banks cannot afford to show artificial losses constantly, because it will be against their own interest in many respects. It is true that even after taking all such precautions, there will remain a possibility of some cases where dishonest clients may succeed in their evil designs, but the punitive steps and the general atmosphere of the business will gradually reduce the number of such cases. (Even in an interest-based economy, the defaulters have always been creating the problem of bad debts). But it should not be taken as a justification, or as an excuse, for rejecting the whole system of Musharakah.

Back to Top

Mudarabahah Transaction

218. Moreover, Islamic banking is not restricted to profit and loss sharing. Though Musharakah is the ideal mode of financing that fully conforms, not only to the principles of Islamic jurisprudence, but also to the basic philosophy of an Islamic economy,

yet there is a variety of instruments that may be used on the assets side of the bank, like Murabahah, leasing, salam, istisna, etc. Some of these models are less risky and may be adopted where Musharakah has abnormal risks or is not applicable to a particular transaction. Some of the appellants have complained that the Federal Shariat Court, in its impugned judgment, has declared the mark-up system, too, as against the injunctions of Islam. It means that Murabahah cannot be used by an Islamic bank as a permissible mode of financing.

219. This complaint is misconceived. The Federal Shariat Court has not held the Murabahah transaction as invalid in principle. It has rather suggested Murabahah for financing exports in para 367 of its judgment. However, the Court has held the "mark-up system as in vogue" to be against the Islamic injunctions and has expressed its apprehension that this mode will be subject to misuse and, applied without fulfilling the necessary conditions on a large scale basis, it will bring little difference to the present system. We have already observed that the "mark-up system as in vogue in Pakistan" is not a Murabahah transaction in the least. It is merely a change of name. The purported sale of goods never takes place in real terms. If Murabahah is effected with all its necessary conditions, it is not impermissible in Shar'iah, nor has the Federal Court declared it as an absolutely impermissible transaction per se. We have already mentioned above while describing the background of the objection of the infidels against the prohibition of *riba* that "sale is similar to *riba* " (in paras 50 and 51 of this judgment) that they used to sell a commodity on deferred payment for a higher

price. Their objection was that when they increase the price at the initial stage of sale, it has not been held as prohibited but when the purchaser fails to pay on the due date, and they claim an additional amount for giving him more time, it is termed as "*riba*" and haram. The Holy Qur'an answered this objection by saying: "Allah has allowed sale and forbidden *riba*." As explained earlier (in para 190 of this judgment) Murabahah is a sale and not a financing in its origin. It must, therefore, conform to all the basic standards of a sale. It may be used only where the client of the bank really wants to purchase a commodity. The bank must purchase it from the original supplier and after taking into its ownership and (physical or constructive) possession sells it to the client. All these elements must be visibly present in a valid Murabahah with all their legal and logical consequences, including in particular, that the bank must assume the risk of the commodity so long as it remains in its ownership and possession. This is the basic feature of the Murabahah which makes it distinct from an interest-based financing and once it is ignored, though for the purpose of simplicity, the whole transaction steps into the prohibited field of interest-based financing.

220. An objection frequently raised against a Murabahah transaction is that when used as a mode of financing it contemplates an increased price based on the deferred payment. It means that the price of commodity in a Murabahah transaction is more than the price of the same commodity in spot market. Since the price is increased against the time given to the purchaser, it resembles the interest-based loan transaction.

221. We have already explained in para 136 to 140 of this judgment that Islam has treated money and commodity differently. Having different characteristics both are subject to different rules and principles. Since money has no intrinsic utility, but is only a medium of exchange which has no different qualities, the exchange of a unit of money for another unit of the same denomination cannot be effected except at par value. If a currency note of Rs.1000/= is exchanged for another note of Pakistani rupees, it must be of the value of R.1000/= . The price of the former note can neither be increased nor decreased from Rs.1000/= even in a spot transaction, because the currency note has no intrinsic utility nor a different quality (recognized legally), therefore, any excess on either side is without consideration, hence, not allowed in Shar'iah. As this is true in a spot exchange transaction, it is also true in a credit transaction where there is money on both sides, because if some excess is claimed in a credit transaction (where money is exchanged for money) it will be against nothing but time.

222. The case of normal commodities is different. Since they have intrinsic utility and have different qualities, the owner is at liberty to sell them at whatever price he wants, subject to the forces of supply and demand. If the seller does not commit a fraud or misrepresentation, he can sell a commodity at a price higher than the market rate with the consent of the purchaser. If the purchaser accepts to buy it at that increased price, the excess charged from him is quite permissible for the seller. When the seller can sell his commodity at a higher price in a cash transaction, he can also charge a higher price

in a credit sale, subject only to the condition that he neither deceives the purchaser, nor compels him to purchase, and the buyer agrees to pay the price with his free will.

223. It is sometimes argued that the increase of price in a cash transaction is not based on the deferred payment, therefore, it is permissible while in a sale based on deferred payment, the increase is purely against time which makes it analogous to interest. This argument is again based on the misconception that whenever price is increased, taking the time of payment into consideration, the transaction comes within the definition of interest. This presumption is not correct. Any excess amount charged against late payment is *riba* only where the subject matter is money on both sides. But if a commodity is sold in exchange of money, the seller, when fixing the price, may take into consideration different factors, including the time of payment. A seller, being the owner of a commodity which has intrinsic utility may charge a higher price and the purchaser may agree to pay it due to various reasons for example:

> (a) His shop is nearer to the buyer who does not want to go to the market which is not so near.

> (b) The seller is more trust-worthy for the purchaser than others, and the purchaser has more confidence in him that he will give him the required thing without any defect.

(c) The seller gives him priority in selling commodities having more demand.

(d) The atmosphere of the shop of the seller is cleaner and more comfortable than other shops.

(e) The seller is more courteous in his dealings than others.

224. These and similar other consideration play their role in charging a higher price from the customer. In the same way, if a seller increases the price because he allows credit to his client, it is not prohibited by Shar'iah if there is no cheating and the purchaser accepts it with open eyes, because whatever the reason of increase, the whole price is against a commodity and not against money. It is true that while increasing the price of the commodity, the seller has kept in view the time of its payment but once the price is fixed, it relates to the commodity, and not to the time, the price will remain the same and can never be increased by the seller. Had it been against time, it might have been increased, if the seller allows him more time after the maturity.

225. To put it another way, since money can only be traded in at par value, as explained earlier, any excess claimed in a credit transaction (of money in exchange of money) is against nothing but time. That is why if the debtor is allowed more time at maturity, some more money is claimed from him. Conversely, in a credit sale of a commodity, time is not the exclusive consideration while fixing the

price. The price is fixed for commodity, not for time. However, time may act as an ancillary factor to determine the price of the commodity, like any other factor from those mentioned above, but once this factor has played its role, every part of the price is attributed to the commodity.

226. The upshot of this discussion is that when money is exchanged for money, no excess is allowed, neither in cash transaction, nor in credit, but where a commodity is sold for money, the price agreed upon by the parties may be higher than the market price, both in cash and credit transactions. Time of payment may act as an ancillary factor to determine the price of a commodity, but it cannot act as an exclusive basis for and the whole consideration of an excess claimed in exchange of money for money.

227. This position is accepted unanimously by all the four schools of Islamic law and the majority of the Muslim jurists. This is the correct legal position of Murabahah transaction according to Shar'iah. However, two points must be remembered:

> a) The Murabahah when used as a mode of trade financing is borderline transaction with very fine lines of distinction as compared to an interest bearing loan. These fine lines of distinction can be observed only when all the basic requirements already explained are fully complied with. To ignore any one of them makes it an interest-bearing financing, therefore, it should always

be effected with due care and precaution.

b) Notwithstanding the permissibility of the Murabahah transaction, it is susceptible to misuse and keeping in view the basic philosophy of an Islamic financial system it is not an ideal way of financing. Hence it should be used only where the Musharakah and Mudarabah are not applicable.

228. Apart from Musharakah and Mudarabah there are other modes of financing like Ijara (Leasing), Salam and Istisna that can be used in different types of financing. We need not go into the details of these because they are elaborated in different reports submitted to the government for the elimination of Interest. The first comprehensive report in this respect was submitted by the Council of Islamic Ideology in 1980. The second report was that of the Commission for Islamization of Economy, constituted under the Shariat Act. This Commission has submitted its comprehensive report to the government in 1991. Lastly, the same Commission was reconstituted under the Chairmanship of Raja Zafarul Haq which submitted its final report in August 1997. We have gone through all these reports and without commenting on each and every detail proposed in them we are satisfied that all these reports can at least be taken as the basic ground work for bringing about the change in our present financial system.

229. The upshot of this discussion is that the Doctrine of Necessity cannot be applied to protect the present interest based system for ever or for an indefinite period. However, this doctrine can be availed of for allowing a reasonable time to the government necessarily required for the switch-over to an interest-free Islamic financial system.

Back to Top

The Loans of the Government

230. One major difficulty in the process of elimination of Interest is felt to be the borrowings of the Government. At present the government of Pakistan is heavily indebted to domestic and foreign lenders. So far as the domestic loans are concerned, their conversion to Islamic modes of financing has been discussed in detail in all the reports referred to above. Dr. Waqar Masood Khan, Vice president of International Islamic University, Islamabad, appearing as a juris-consult in this case, has also discussed the magnitude of the problem and has thoroughly examined the ramifications of elimination of Interest from this sector. In his statement submitted to the Court he has discussed this issue from page 29 to 49. The substance of the alternative suggestions is that all the borrowings of the government from domestic sources should be designed on the basis of project-related financing. This will, in addition to being compatible with Shar'iah, help curbing the corruption and misappropriation of borrowed funds. After examining all this material we are of the view that in this sector too, the interest cannot be taken as a necessity to continue for an indefinite period.

However, this area may justify some more time for transformation than the private banking transactions will require.

Back to Top

Foreign Loans

231. Although the laws under challenge in the present case are not specifically related to the foreign borrowings, yet it is obvious that once the interest is held illegal, these transactions will also be hit by the prohibition in some way or the other. This seems to be the most difficult area where the prohibition of interest is required to be implemented. The government's foreign loans as of 1 March 1999 stand at $31.15 billion or Rs.1610 billion at the current interbank rate. It is argued that conversion of this type of borrowing to an interest-free basis is almost impossible.

232. Before we touch upon the Islamic solution to this problem we would like to observe that the speed at which our foreign borrowings are increasing merits serious consideration. In the beginning we started borrowing funds from international sources for our development projects. Later the scope of foreign borrowing was extended even to the non-development expenses. Thereafter huge amounts were borrowed for debt servicing and now these borrowings are meant to pay interest to the international lenders.

233. It needs no expertise in economics to realize that this is an alarming situation which is leading constantly towards the slavery of the whole nation

in the hands of our lenders. We are mortgaging the future of our present and coming generations by incurring huge debts every year. The notion that the foreign borrowings help the developing countries in their development projects and assist in attaining prosperity is now proved to be false in the case of a large number of the "third world" countries. This fact is increasingly realized by the independent economists. Susan George, an American economist living in France has written widely on development and world issues. She is an Associate Director of the Transnational Institute in Amsterdam and her books on the Third World debt have been widely admired, some of which have won international awards. She has summarized the eye-opening results of the Third World debt in the following words:

> "According to the OECD, between 1982 and 1990, total resource flows to developing countries amounted to $927 billion. This sum includes the OECD categories of Official Development Finance, Export Credits and Private Flows - in other words, all official bilateral and multilateral aid, grants by private charities, trade credits plus direct private investment and bank loans. Much of this inflow was not in the form of grants but was rather new debt, on which dividends or interest will naturally come due in future.
>
> During the same 1982-90 period, developing countries remitted in debt

service alone 1342 billion (interest and principal) to the creditor countries. For a true picture of resource flows, one would have to add many other South-to-North outflows, such as royalties, dividends, repatriated profits, underpaid raw materials and the like. The income-outflow difference between $1345 and $927 billion is thus a much understated $418 billion in the rich countries' favor. For purposes of comparison, the US Marshall Plan transferred $14 billion 1948 dollars to war-ravaged Europe, about $70 billion in 1991 dollars. Thus in the eight years from 1982-90 the poor have financed six Marshall Plans for the rich through debt service alone.

Have these extraordinary outflows at least served to reduce the absolute size of the debt burden? Unfortunately not. In spite of total debt service, including amortization, of more than 1.3 trillion dollars from 1982-90, the debtor countries as a group began the 1990s fully 61 percent more in debt than they were in 1982. Sub-Saharan Africa's debt increased by 113 per cent during this period; the debt burden of the very purest - the so-called 'LLDCs' or 'least developed' countries - was up by 110 per cent."

Many neutral writers are of the view that Third World debt is not just a financial matter, but a political one. There were always severe conditions attached to IMF and World Bank loans. Although "program aid" required borrowing nations to conform to a package of economic and social expenditure measures aimed to ensure that funds are used for development, yet when projects failed and debts increased, "program aid" was followed by "structural adjustment" that entailed supervising the development of the entire economy of the indebted countries. Thus the lenders justified their total interference in the domestic policies of the Third World nations. As these policies, too, failed to bring a turnaround in the debt trends, "austerity programs" were introduced whereby expenditure on social services, welfare and education were cut to a considerable extent. Susan George and Fabrizio Sabelli have commented the results of these policies as follows:

> "Between 1980 and 1989 some thirty-three African countries received 241 structural adjustment loans. During that same period, average GDP per capita in those countries fell 1.1% per year, while per capita food production also experienced steady decline. The real value of the minimum wage dropped by over 25%, government expenditure on education fell from $11 billion to $7 billion and primary school enrolments dropped from 80% in 1980 to 69% in 1990. The number of poor people in these

countries rose from 184 million in 1985 to 216 million in 1990, an increase of seventeen per cent."

234. According to the assessment of the World Bank itself, which is subjected to serious doubts by some economists, the success rate of World-Bank-funded projects has been less than 50%. In addition, after a review in 1989, World Bank staff were unable to point out a single project in which the displaced people had been relocated and rehabilitated to a standard of living comparable to that which they enjoyed before displacement.

235. Even the successful projects did seldom bring an overall economic well-being of the indebted countries. Michael Rowbotham says:

> "There has been a massive outpouring of literature on the subject of Third World debt. The books are characterized by one feature. Whereass the arguments and policies of the IMF and World Bank have been based upon an apparently reasonable theory, the studies give case after case and country after country, in which the theory has not worked in practice. Either loans have led to development, but repayment has proved impossible; or the projects funded have failed completely leaving the country with a massive debt and no hope of repayment, or repeated additional loans have become necessary simply

to provide funds for the repayment of past loans. The debtor countries, as a group, began the 1990s fully 61% deeper in debt than they were in 1980."

Many critics have compared the Third World debt with peonage or wage slavery. Cheryl Payer observes:

"The system can be compared point by point with peonage on an individual scale. In the peonage, or debt slavery system... the aim of the employer/creditor/merchant is neither to collect the debt once and for all, nor to starve the employee to death, but rather to keep the laborer permanently indentured through his debt to the employer... Precisely the same system operates on the international level... It is debt slavery on an international scale. If they remain within the system, the debtor countries are doomed to perpetual underdevelopment or rather, to development of their exports at the service of multinational enterprises, at the expense of development for the needs of their own citizens."

236. In 1987, the conference of the Institute for African Alternatives called for the winding up of the World Bank and the IMF and a complete end to the dominance of the Bretton Woods International

monetary system. The conference noted the results of the case studies as follows:

> "In virtually all cases, the impact of these (IMF and World Bank) projects has been basically negative. They have resulted in massive unemployment, falling real incomes, pernicious inflation, increased imports with persistent trade deficits, net outflow of capital, mounting external debts, denial of basic needs, severe hardship and deindustrialization. Even the so-called success stories in Ghana and the Ivory Coast have turned out to offer no more than temporary relief which had collapsed by the mid 1980s. The sectors that have been worst hit are agriculture, manufacturing and the social services, while the burden of adjustment has fallen regressively on the poor and weak social groups."

237. These facts should be sufficient to realize fallacy of the illusionary notions that the Third World countries cannot live without the help of foreign loans. Who has, in fact, benefited from this system? This question is closely examined by a Canadian scholar Jaques B. Gelinas in his book "Freedom From Debt". He says:

> "The foreign-aid-based development model has proved itself powerless to bring a single country out of

economic and financial dependence. However, it has turned out to be a source of fabulous wealth for certain Third World elites, giving birth to a new form of power and a socio-political class that can rightly be called the 'aidocracy.'"

The case of Pakistan is not much different. At a time when we are in the dire need to improve the economic status of our people, to eradicate poverty, to raise the level of our education, and to provide at least the minimum health requirements to our rural areas where thousands of men, women and children are at the brink of death for want of any medical aid, we are forced to allocate 46% of our total budget for repayment of interest-based loans. Still, we are striving to acquire more loans to pay off some of the previous ones. When these new loans will mature, we will have to incur more debts to satisfy some of the present liabilities. How far can we proceed in this vicious circle? How long shall we keep coiling around the spiral of loans over loans? We will have to get rid of this debt-based economy which has usurped our freedom and has pawned our next generations in the hands of our lenders. This is a question of life-and-death for our nation, and we will have to resolve it at any cost.

238. We are not oblivious of the fact that once thrust into the present state of indebtedness, we cannot free ourselves from it overnight. It will require a well-considered program and a firm commitment to implement it. In the intervening period, which must be minimized by competent planning, we will have to live with the present state

of indebtedness. But even in this intervening period, we must try our best to renegotiate with our lenders to convert the existing loans into Islamic modes of financing. Thanks to the atmosphere created by the Islamic banking, these modes of financing are no longer totally unfamiliar to the West. Even the International financial institutions have undertaken studies to understand them. IFC, the private financing branch of the World Bank has already expressed its willingness to use some Islamic modes of financing. The assets-related loans can easily be converted into Leasing arrangement. Project related loans can be reshaped on the basis of Istisna. The concern of the lenders is to get return on their loans, and not to insist on a particular form. Therefore, it should not be much difficult to renegotiate the existing loans on Islamic lines. For new finances even wider variety of modes is available that can be designed on the basis of Islamic principles. However, it will be possible only if the government itself has a firm commitment to its Islamic obligations and a true will to implement what Islam requires. An apologetic attitude can never convince others to bring change in the long-practiced ideas. Embarrassing for the whole nation are the remarks of the President of IFC (International Finance Corporation, an affiliate of the World Bank) in his report to the Board of Directors of IFC about a proposed investment in the Hala Spinning Mills. He observed:

> "A change to Islamic modes of financing has been considered by IFC, but this would be contrary to the Government (of Pakistan's) intentions for foreign loans.

> Adoption by a foreign lender of Islamic instruments could be construed as undermining Government's policy to exempt foreign lenders from this requirement."

239. On November 17, 1990, the Prime Minister of Pakistan had appointed a committee of experts to analyze the growing dependence of our country on foreign assistance and to chalk out a plan to reduce this dependence and evolve a self-reliance development strategy. The committee, headed by the then Senator Prof. Khurshid Ahmad, comprised the Secretary finance division and the Chief economist of the economic division and several other economic experts. The report of the Committee was submitted to the government in April 1991. This Committee, after deliberations, came to the conclusion that even on pure economic grounds, the goal of self-reliance can be achieved only by elimination of interest. The recommendations of this committee can be availed of while tackling with the issue of foreign loans.

240. Therefore, the admitted difficulties in resolving the problem of foreign liabilities cannot be taken as an excuse for exempting them from the prohibition for good or for an indefinite period on the basis of necessity. However, it cannot be denied that it will take more time than the domestic transactions. The doctrine of necessity will be applicable to this extent only.

My Comments 20: Since Islam does not prohibit Interest, as such, the question of applying the doctrine of necessity to retain the system based thereon does not arise.

While discussing this doctrine, however, the learned Judge has again blamed Interest for the debt trap, the developing countries have fallen into. He seems to suggest that once Interest is prohibited, the malaise will come to an end, albeit slowly.

I have to repeat that it is a case of wrong diagnosis by the learned Judge. Unless and until a country like Pakistan effectively changes its corrupt way of life, there is no hope of its ever coming out of the vicious debt trap. <u>A change to the so-called Islamic modes, even for getting foreign loans, will entail a much greater control of the foreign creditors over the internal affairs of the country.</u> These foreign creditors, as one of the reports quoted by the learned Judge suggests, would have their own self-interest and may perpetuate the peonage or debt slavery system in some form or the other.

Prohibition of misapprpriation of other people's rightful dues, by all fraudulent and dishonest means like gambling (speculating) in shares or issuing loans on baseless money is the panacea for all the economic ills. In other words, the panacea is the strict implementation of the divine injunction against the real *Ar-Riba,* as defined in the Qur'aan!

Back to Top

Conclusions

241. The upshot of the above discussion is that:

242. Any additional amount over the principal in a contract of loan or debt is the *riba* prohibited by the Holy Qur'an in several verses. The Holy Prophet, Sall-Allahu alayhi wa sallam, has also termed the following transactions as *riba*:

> (i) A transaction of money for money of the same denomination where the quantity on both sides is not equal, either in a spot transaction or in a transaction based on deferred payment.

> (ii) A barter transaction between two weighable or measurable commodities of the same kind, where the quantity on both sides is not equal, or where the delivery from any one side is deferred.

> (iii) A barter transaction between two different weighable or measurable commodities where delivery from one side is deferred.

243. These three categories are termed in the Islamic jurisprudence as *riba* -al-sunnah because their prohibition is established by the Sunnah of the Holy Prophet, Sall-Allahu alayhi wa sallam. Along with the *riba* -al-Qur'an, these are four types of transactions termed as ' *riba* ' in the literature of Islamic fiqh based on the Holy Qur'an and Sunnah.

244. Out of these four transactions, the last two ones, mentioned above as (ii) and (iii) have not much relevance to the context of modern business, the barter business being a rare phenomenon in the modern trade. However, the *riba* -al-Qur'an, and transaction of money mentioned above as (i) are more relevant to modern business.

245. In the light of the detailed discussion above, there is no difference between different types of loan, so far as the prohibition of *riba* is concerned. It also does not make any difference whether the additional amount stipulated over the principal loan or debt is small or large. It is, therefore, held that all the prevailing forms of interest, either in the banking transactions or in private transactions do fall within the definition of "*riba* ." Similarly, any interest stipulated in the government borrowings, acquired from domestic or foreign sources, is *riba* and clearly prohibited by the Holy Qur'an.

246. The present financial system, based on interest, is against the injunctions of Islam as laid down by the Holy Qur'an and Sunnah, and in order to bring it in conformity with Shar'iah, it has to be subjected to radical changes.

247. A variety of Islamic modes of financing have been developed by Islamic scholars, economists and bankers that may serve as a better alternative to interest. These modes are being practiced by about 200 Islamic financial institutions in different parts of the world.

248. These alternatives being available, the transactions of interest cannot be allowed to

continue for ever on the basis of necessity. Many experienced bankers, to name a few such as Dr. Ahmad Muhammad Ali, President Islamic Development Bank, Jeddah, Mr. Adnan al-Bahr, Chief Executive International Investor, Kuwait, Mr. Iqbal Ahmad Khan, Chief executive Islamic unit of the Hong Kong Shanghai Banking Corporation (HSBC) based in London from outside Pakistan and Mr. Abdul-Jabbar Khan, the former president of the National Bank of Pakistan, Mr. Shahid Hasan Siddiqui and Mr. Maqbool Ahmad Khan from Pakistan are the bankers who have a long experience of banking in different parts of the world, besides others appeared before us. All of them were unanimous on the point that Islamic modes of financing are not only feasible, but area also more beneficial to bring about a balanced and stable economy, for which they have produced detailed proof based on facts and figures. Some outstanding economists like Dr. Umar Chapra, the economic advisor to Saudi Monetary Agency, Dr. Arshad Zaman, the former Chief economist of the ministry of Finance government of Pakistan, Prof. Khurshid Ahmad, Dr. Nawab Hyder Naqwi, Dr. Waqar Masood Khan, have supported this view in their detailed discourses.

249. We have also gone through the detailed reports of the council of Islamic Ideology submitted in 1980, the report of the commission for Islamization of Economy constituted in 1991, and the final report of the same commission, reconstituted in 1997 which was submitted in August 1997. We have also perused the report of the Prime Minister's Committee on Self-Reliance, submitted to the Government in April 1991.

250. There is thus ample evidence to prove that quite a substantial ground work has been done to suggest the strategy for the transformation of the existing financial system to the Islamic one, and the present interest based system cannot be retained for an indefinite period on the basis of necessity. However, the transformation may take some time which can be allowed on that basis.

251. For the reasons given above, all these appeals are hereby dismissed in the terms detailed hereafter in the Order of the Court.

My Conclusions: It makes me sad to note that a renowned Islamic scholar and Judge of the Supreme Court of an Islamic country has based his Judgement on a falsehood. He has based this Judgement of his on the premise that the Qur'aan has not defined 'Ar-Riba' that is specifically prohibited by Allah.

This is a false premise, as verse 30.39 does define the Qur'aanic term as it (the very same verse) also defines 'Az-Zakaat'! Subsequently revealed Qur'aanic verses on 'Ar-Riba' give further elaboration of the basic concept of the term given in verse 30.39.

'Ar-Riba', as so defined, is the increase sought in a transaction by usurping other people's rightfully owned properties, earnings and dues ('amwaal').

Interest, per se, constitutes proportional expenses incurred plus proportional reasonable profit earned by a financial institution for making the purchasing power (money) available to those who need it. Interest, as such, (so far as it is restricted to recovery of expenses and reasonable profit) is the rightful 'amwaal' of the institution and not of other people. It is therefore NOT 'Ar-Riba'!

The quick buck, earned by the banks by adopting dubious means, like speculating in the share market and issuing loans on baseless money, is, on the other hand, 'Ar-Riba'. And it is this 'Ar-Riba' that has brought about the appalling condition of our present financial system.

To get ourselves free of this sorry state, we must implement honestly the injunction on 'Ar-Riba' as defined by Allah, and not as wrongly defined by His creatures.

Developing countries can get out of the vicious debt trap only if they change their corrupt way of life. Their corruption is the real 'Ar-Riba'! To describe honest interest, per se, as 'Ar-Riba' is a lie.

As the Qur'aan says, "Look, how they invent the lie **against** Allah! And this is enough to constitute a sin, manifest." [Q: 4.50]

Comments by
Mohammad Shafi

www.ingramcontent.com/pod-product-compliance
Lightning Source LLC
Chambersburg PA
CBHW030624220526
45463CB00004B/1410